The Diary

Ada Jackson

1883

A Living History Unit Publication

ISBN 0901 675 059
© M. M. Blow 1993
Published by Leicester City Council
Living History Unit

Contents

Introduction

This is the diary kept by Ada Jackson for the year commencing 1 January 1883, when she was 19 years old. It was handwritten by her in a foolscap "scribbling diary" supplied by Rowe and Sons, printers and stationers of Granby Street, Leicester, from which we also learn that a dog licence cost 7s 6d (37.5 pence), that playing cards carried an import duty of 3s 9d (18 pence) per dozen packs, and that the standard rate of income tax in 1882-3 was 5d (2 pence) in the pound.

Ada was born on 19 March 1863, the only child of John Thomas Jackson of Leicester, and his wife Mary Ann. The family lived at 9 Pares Street, one of a cluster of streets laid out in the 1830s and 1840s in the northern part of the town, between St. Margaret's Church and the Leicester Canal. The street was demolished earlier this century.

Hard-working, sober and thrifty, this was a "respectable" and relatively affluent working class household. "Father had to come home from work this morning, he has to be very bad to do that", notes Ada one day; though on another, "I do feel idle this day..... I should like a holiday.... ain't I a bad girl". John Jackson enjoyed a drink - Ada was occasionally sent to "fetch the ale" - but never to excess. "I am so sorry", writes Ada of one acquaintance, "we found her in so much trouble about her husband, he drinks so sometimes and then comes home and ill uses her". The piano and washing machine, the outings to the theatre, the day trips to the coast, and even the subscriptions to "Father's Club" - presumably a Friendly Society or similar organisation - were still well beyond the means of many working class families at this time.

John Jackson's occupation was given as "foreman" in 1884, but as the diary suggests, he also owned two houses in Chestnut Street, off the Aylestone Road. On one occasion Ada had to "go of an errand for Father to fetch the rents", while on another, George Beecroft, the young man around whom much of Ada's diary revolves, "told Father he would mend the window sashes down Chestnut Street".

George was a carpenter and joiner by trade. Originally from South Witham in Lincolnshire, in 1874 he was apprenticed for four years to the firm of George and John Thomas Thorp, elastic web manufacturers, of Friday Street in Leicester. This was close to Pares Street itself, as was the anonymous "Factory" to which Ada refers, and it seems likely that both George and Ada's father were employed at Thorp's during the period covered by the diary.

Unlike many of those employed in Leicester at this time, both he and George appear to have enjoyed regular work with a regular income - arguably a more important factor in maintaining a comfortable lifestyle than the level of wages themselves. In 1881 almost 45% of the working population of the town was employed in clothing manufacture, the majority in the footwear and hosiery industries. Both were much subject to seasonal "boom and bust" cycles culminating in lay-offs and short-time work.

In many households male wages were insufficient to support the family, and those of its female members were essential to maintaining a reasonable standard of living. Beyond an occasional hint of some dressmaking at home - "Mrs Twigger sent the money for that cape last night, it has been done about twelve months, 'Better Late than Never' " - it is not clear from the diary whether Ada's mother Mary Ann did any paid work. Ada herself worked at the firm of Thomas Webster and Co., hat and cap manufacturers, in East Bond Street. The company - motto "Labor Omnia Vincit" or "Work Conquers All" - produced not only silk, felt and tweed hats, but police helmets, and embroidered caps for schools, colleges and sporting activities, many of them exported to Europe or the Colonies.

Cap manufacture was largely a female occupation. According to a description of Webster's in 1891, "a small army of young women are busily cutting, quartering and sewing together all manner of caps, with linings and ornamental attachments complete. Here, too are a multitude of machines doing 3000 stitches per minute, and keeping up a continuous whirr, while the busy fingers which manage them are fitting, piecing and finishing the 1000 odd patterns of caps which the firm is turning out".

Ada was employed on piecework, so her wages were always subject to fluctuation. Her highest weekly earnings in the course of 1883 were 13s 8d (68 pence) : "more money than I have ever got in my life.... I must not get too much, or I will have my work docked". Information about wage rates from this period is rather sparse, but in the mid 1880s the national average of female wages in the hosiery industry was around 11s 6d (57.5 pence); the average for all female occupations around 12s 8d (63 pence), compared with 24s 7d (£1. 23) for males*.

However, Ada rarely enjoyed the same regularity of work as her father. "I had another half day's holiday this afternoon, I am ashamed of the money I earn", she noted in a typical entry in February. In July, "we had a half day's holiday, short of work again", while in December, "There is another gross of smoking caps ordered, we are quite busy..... we are generally short at this time of the year".

There were compensations, nonetheless - not least the company of her close friend Elly, and the opportunity to talk over matters of moment with her while at work. "Elly and I have been gabbing again this morning", as she wrote in one entry, "we try to keep silent for a little while (but) it is a struggle". In common with other major employers in the later 19th century, Thomas Webster also gave his workforce an annual summer "treat", consisting in 1883 of a railway excursion to Skegness.

Despite the fluctuating fortunes of individual industries, by the 1880s Leicester was enjoying a prosperity which contrasted sharply with the first half of the 19th century. Between 1851 and 1881 the population of the town doubled to 122,000, growing by 40% in the 1860s alone - a rate of increase which, in the words of the Registrar-General in 1871, "can hardly be matched", and which reflected new openings for employment in the town.

*British Labour Statistics : Historical Abstract, 1886 - 1968

New industrial development and the boost it gave to existing industry were at the root of this expansion. Until the 1850s, the hosiery industry - still based largely in homes or small workshops - was Leicester's only substantial industry. So heavily did the town depend on it, that economic depression had widespread and often tragic effects. "Food dear, employment at an end, and the weather often very severe, vast numbers suffered greatly", the town's Unitarian Domestic Missionary, Joseph Dare, noted tersely in 1848.

From the 1850s, aided by its central position on the national railway network, Leicester developed into a major centre of footwear manufacture and distribution. As in the hosiery, much work was initially done in the home or small workshop. However, not only did footwear manufacture soak up surplus male labour from the hosiery, creating new openings in the latter for women, it provided a much-needed stimulus to the hosiery industry itself: to the manufacture of elastic webbing, for instance, much in demand for boots as well as gloves, stocking tops, and a range of other garments.

Such household names as Corah, Stead and Simpson and George Oliver were well-established by the 1880s. As both industries broadened their markets and became more reliant on mechanisation and factory production, specialist firms grew up locally to meet their needs: cardboard box manufacturers, for instance, and engineering firms like Pearson and Bennion, forerunner of the British United Shoe Machinery Company. Even so, mechanisation was a gradual process, more easily applied to cutting and stitching than to many other processes, and still often dependent on manual rather than steam power. It is "hard work treadling", as Ada said of the embroidery machinery she used at Webster's; but "I am going to have the embroidery stitch of my Wilcocks and Gibbs machine made larger.....it is to go by steam, I shall like that, it will not be such hard work".

PASSPORTS.

An Englishman travelling on the Continent seldom needs a Passport, except in war times; but it is nevertheless *advisable* to carry one, as it is at all times proof of identity. A Passport is *necessary* for Austria, Egypt, Greece, Portugal, Russia, and Turkey, and is occasionally demanded in Germany and Spain. Travellers intending to visit Russia are advised to have their passport visé before starting. Passports are issued to British-born subjects by the various British Consuls abroad on personal application, or in London on presentation of a recommendation from a Banker *under seal*, or upon the production of a Certificate of Identity, signed by a Magistrate, Clergyman, Physician, Solicitor, Notary, or M.P., and countersigned by the person on whose behalf the Certificate is granted. Passports are issued to naturalised British subjects only on *personal* application at the Foreign Office. The charge for issue of a Passport is 2/, and for Visas—Belgium 3/6, France 9/, Germany 3/, Greece 11/, Holland 3/6, Italy 5/, Portugal 5/9, Russia 3/, Spain 5/6, Switzerland 3/.

Letts, Son, and Co., Limited, obtain Passports and Visas on the shortest notice. Write for full particulars.

Rowe's Diary, extract from printed information, 1883 *(Mrs M. Blow)*

As the population of Leicester grew, so did its built-up area. In the earlier 19th century, most growth took place to the east and south of the centre. The River Soar, much given to flooding, was a barrier to the north, while to the west expansion was limited by the Westcotes and Danet's Hall estates, which remained in private hands until after mid-century.

Although Leicester suffered little of the overcrowding seen in many urban areas, mortality rates in the 1840s were notoriously high by comparison with other industrial towns. They began to fall from the 1870s, and by the end of the century were below the national average, but epidemic diseases remained prevalent, and Ada herself suffered a bout of the "English cholera", a regular feature of the summer and winter months.

Otherwise, with the exception of Mary Ann's headaches, and the occasional toothache, the family appeared to enjoy remarkably good health. This may be due in part to the sanitary reforms introduced from mid-century by the Borough Corporation; but declining mortality rates also owed a great deal to the rising standard of living enjoyed by at least some sections of the population in Leicester, and the access it gave them to decent housing and an adequate diet. As the Medical Officer of Health observed in the early 20th century, poverty was "most detrimental to health", and ill health was in turn a major cause of poverty.

After 1874 Leicester was served by a system of horse trams, albeit limited to a few of the main thoroughfares. It was still small enough to be walked with ease, and as Ada's diary suggests, walking - or the "promenading" which enabled a mutual inspection of the sexes - were popular pastimes in themselves. Leicester was well-provided with open spaces even before the opening of the more formal Abbey Park in 1882, foremost among them Freeman's Common, and the old Racecourse, which is now Victoria Park. Beyond the town itself were miles of open countryside, and that most popular local resort, Bradgate Park.

Much of the town's social life was still centred on its public houses and street corners, but there was no lack of other entertainment. The annual fairs in May and October were a long-established feature of the calendar, though in Ada's view, "there don't seem to be half the fun there used to be". There were two theatres in Leicester at this time, in addition to the Floral Hall in Belgrave Gate, which opened in 1876 and staged concerts and theatrical performances as well as exhibitions and other events. The Theatre Royal, in Horsefair Street, was built in 1836, but Ada normally attended the Royal Opera House in Silver Street. Opened in 1877 with seating for over 2500 people, it was in one view "rather beyond the immediate requirements of Leicester" - but "in a few years will prove no defect but an advantage, if we continue to add tens of thousands to our population".

A seat in the Gallery cost 6d (2.5 pence), but the lectures which Ada and her friends attended at the Town Museum and the Temperance Hall were normally free of charge. "An Hour with the Modern Microscope", "The Evidence of the Antiquity of Man", "King John and the Magna Carta", Shakespeare's "As You Like It" - the range of subjects was wonderfully wide, and much in keeping with the Victorian ideal of self-improvement through education.

The lectures themselves attracted large audiences. Ada's own enthusiasm for them may have owed something to the fact that George Beecroft was usually in the audience. However, her obvious interest and enjoyment also suggest a degree of intellectual curiosity, and a sufficiently high standard of education to grasp the subject matter. The diary itself reinforces this impression. Her grammar is occasionally eccentric, her punctuation non-existent in parts, but this gives the text an immediacy which a more "correct" style might lack, and her standard of literacy is still higher than the average that might be expected of a working class woman at this time.

In Leicester, as elsewhere, there was an expansion in educational provision following the 1870 Education Act and the establishment of local School Boards. Voluntary schools existed well before this, however, and it seems likely that Ada attended St. Margaret's Church School. Much of her social life certainly revolved around St. Margaret's - as did George's around his own church, St. Matthew's - but Ada seemed to have her doubts about religion itself. "She believes in GOD", she writes of a friend, but "I tell her she has not had her belief shaken as I have at home".

Ada's relationship with her parents, like their relationship with each other, did not always run smoothly. "I expected Father would take Mother and I out this afternoon", she wrote on Easter Monday, "but I soon found my mistake out, he went marching out alone, I did feel hurt". On another occasion, "I have had a good cry this dinner time because Father has been blowing Mother up about a paltry piece of fish, I feel so sorry for her". Ada herself was not the most placid of people, as she freely admitted. "Oh if I can but keep my temper through the coming year how pleased I shall be", she writes in the very first entry of the diary, but only two days later, "I am afraid my temper has been ruffled a great deal today..... I wish I did not snap at Mother and Father so".

Ada's expectations of herself and her parents were perhaps unreasonably high. The overall impression left by the diary is of an affectionate, supportive and protective family, with a wide circle of friends and acquaintances - but what of Ada's relationship with George, which occupies so much of the diary?

Her dilemma was by no means novel, nor unique to the 1880s. "How are you to know when one is truly in love?", asked one correspondent of the advice column of the "Family Herald" in 1893. "A simple answer is beyond human ingenuity....", was the reply, but "obviously it is easier to know whether you love than to know whether you are loved..... Your readings of another person's heart must always be mixed with a certain degree of surmise".

Ada knew her own feelings well enough. "How happy I am, I am in love", she declared in January, but did George feel the same way, and when - if ever - would he declare his "intentions"? "I do not know what to make of him", she wrote more than once: "I wish he would say something. It seems to me as though he is trifling with me" - but if she openly showed her affection for him, would he think her "fast, like my watch"?

If George himself was left to "surmise" a great deal about Ada's feelings, this was due in part to the same anxiety to behave "correctly". "He brought a book for me to read titled 'Courtship and Marriage'.....", she wrote in June. "This is another singular event as I cannot understand", but "there is some good advice in it, I wonder if he is acting on the advice of that book, it looks a great deal like it.....".

The Living History Unit is grateful to Ada Jackson's granddaughter, Mrs M. Blow, for allowing us to publish this diary. Accounts of working class life by the working classes themselves are unusual enough, and those by working class women are rare indeed. However, if the diary offers us a unique insight into life in Victorian Leicester, it is above all a warm human story which can be read and enjoyed in its own right.

Thanks are also due to Mr and Mrs Blow for providing family photographs and additional background information; and to Mr B. Keymer, Mr G. Peck and Leicestershire Museums, Arts & Records Service for the loan of illustrations.

And finally, did the story have a happy ending in the best traditions of Victorian romance? "The suspense is dreadful", wrote Ada towards the diary's end, but the reader need bear it no longer.....Read on!

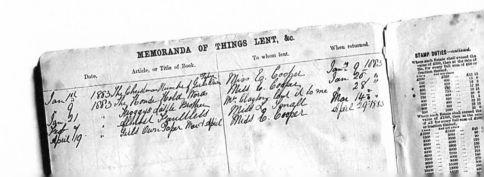

January

Monday January 1st 1883

I will try to begin the New Year as I ought to, today is full of pleasant recollections for me. Had a walk with Miss E. Cooper* in the morning, called to see Mrs Twigger* in the afternoon. Last, but not least, Mr George Beecroft spent the evening with us. Oh, if I can but keep my temper through the coming year, how pleased I shall be, and be as good as possible to every one about me. I had a letter and a Photo from Miss Littlewood, it is very good of her to remember me, I must write back to her.

Tuesday January 2nd

I did not think there was half the pleasure in keeping a diary as there is. I have kept my temper all day, what a battle fought. Started to work today. G. came in for a box of his. How nice it is to write all my secrets down here, and I have partly made those Spill Holders. G. says he will make the bottoms for them.

Wednesday January 3rd

I have been helping Mother wash today, I found out that it is hard work dollying*. Mother bet me a shilling I should want a dolly some day, I bet her I should not. I am afraid my temper has been ruffled a great deal today. How often I thought of you my diary, I try so hard to keep as I should. I wish I did not snap at Mother and Father so, because they are so good to me and seem blind to my faults. I had a walk with Miss L. Small in the evening as far as the Oadby Road*.

*indicates a note on the text

The Museum, New Walk. The central part of the building was originally a school, opened in 1937 *(Leicester City Council)*

Thursday January 4th

I called for Elly in the afternoon to go with me to the Museum*, there was no one at home so I had to go alone. I did feel vexed because I waited some time at Mrs Biggs. I think the Museum is nicely arranged, I shall go again sometime. Elly came down after tea to see whether I had been. I went a little way home with her, and met G. at 7 o'clock. Stayed at home all night.

Friday January 5th

Miss Ross sent for me to go to work in the morning, how aggravating it is to be sent for unexpectedly, I shall be glad when we settle down to work. Father was cross with me this dinnertime, he says I must practice more* or it will be such a waste of money, I am sure I ought to try to please him more than I do.

Saturday January 6th

I had a walk with Elly in the afternoon around the Course and on the Common*. We were very lively at first and had a bit of fun, but of course I got dull coming home. At night I went to meet Elly from the Temperance Hall*, I did not see her after all. Oh, how miserable I felt, I wish I could forget all care and be a bright happy girl. Mother, Father and I had a nice chat at night, he said although he had a nasty tempered girl to deal with, he could manage me. (That dreadful temper of mine).

Sunday 7th January

I had a walk with Father in the morning, I went to school* in the afternoon. Mrs Clayton* wished us all to be as regular in attendance as we could. Elly met me and went to Mrs Biggs to tea. I went to church at night, Mr Lewis* preached, I don't care for his sermons at all. I went for a walk with Elly at night.

Monday January 8th

I felt so dull when I first got to work this morning. I think my happiest time is at work on the whole. At night I went to hear a lecture on "THE EVOLUTION OF THE SOLAR SYSTEM" by Richard A. Proctor, and it was very good too. G. was there behind Elly, I enjoyed it very much. Mr Proctor recited some very pretty poetry after the lecture. I must go to hear the rest of them if I can possibly get*. I wish I was not in such a cloud of wonder as I am.

Tuesday January 9th

Elly and I had a bit of fun this afternoon, we have to cheer ourselves up sometimes. Still unsettled, if my mind was more at rest I should be happier, I lose all hope and get that irritable besides letting them all see at home how unsociable I am. I should not like anyone to read this, they would think I am a very silly girl, but I don't think they will while I keep my desk locked.

Wednesday January 10th

What a lot of fun we have had at work today, my arm tingled again with Elly slapping me. She can thump when she likes and so can I, she says. Lily came down for me tonight, we went for a long walk and had a very sensible talk, her views and mine are very different. I believe I am a silly weak minded girl over young fellows, I try to be perfection, but I don't succeed at all.

Thursday January 11th

My Grandfather Hyde* spent the day with us. Elly is always slapping me, we had about half a dozen fights this afternoon. George came in tonight, he was singing, we managed the "Village Blacksmith" and others better. I did not feel half so shy, we seem to get used to each other. I have been good all this day. I cannot write down what I think as well as I should like, I must do my best and be satisfied.

Friday January 12th

I am beginning to neglect my diary so soon in the New Year, that will not do. I had half a day's holiday this afternoon as it was Friday. I stayed at home and helped Mother clean, she had the headache very bad. I feel more contented than I have done for some time now. I have been trying to make a work basket, don't know how it will look when it is finished, well I must do my best, I can do no more.

Saturday January 13th

Elly told me some news from Annie Freeman, she said her young fellow and George had a long talk last Tuesday evening. G. thought I was very quiet, I should liked to have been behind them when they were talking. He came for dinner and did some work after. Elly came while he was here, I introduced them to each other. I went with Elly to a lecture by Mr Amos - "Common and Uncommon Sayings", it was very good.

Sunday January 14th

I went to school, George was here when I got home, he had tea with us at last. I went to church at night. Mr Clayton* preached a very good sermon, but I did not feel inclined to listen tonight. Down in the dumps again.

Monday January 15th

I am still looking on the dark side of things. Elly says I ought to be happy, but much wants more. G. has left his Church Hymn Book, I should think that means he has got to come in again. I should not like him to read my diary, though it would show him the state of my mind plainly. I was telling Kate how I liked Miss E. Small, she said Ellen liked me. I thought I was too disagreeable for anybody to care for me much. I thought I should not find enough to write down every day, I can generally find plenty on the whole.

Tuesday January 16th

I went to St. Margaret's School*, I met Miss Bella Cooke and was with her all night, I am so glad I went. I enjoyed myself so very much with the games and dancing, it is no use talking, I shall have to go to a class to learn. I feel so vexed to see others dancing and me looking on. Mr G. Baum had me for a partner in one of the games. I shall move to him when I see him now. I shall go next Tuesday to the sewing class.

Wednesday January 17th

I had another half day's holiday this afternoon. I thought how nice it would be to go to see Miss Emery at the school, so I went for Pattie. When I got there I found she was married! Oh I was surprised. She could not go with me to Miss Emery, so I stayed there to tea. Mrs Barrat now, there is another of my friends gone. She says she shall go to see Miss Emery although she is married. At night I had a walk with L. Small for

Abbey Park, programme of Official Opening in 1882,
(Leicester City Council).

about an hour, I called for her and stayed for a short time.

Thursday January 18th

I went to tell Father to come in for his tea. A. Measures* was there, Father was teasing her, she is blind as she cannot see how they mess her. I was weighed; 8 stone, what a lump, I have not lost any flesh this last 12 months. At night I stayed at home and did the ironing. How miserable and lonely I feel today, it must be with seeing Pattie now she is a married woman.

Friday January 19th

Elly and I had a half day's holiday this morning, we went down the Park* for a short while and enjoyed ourselves thoroughly under present circumstances. We were singing and dancing until it began to rain, then we came home and I helped Mother till dinnertime, went to work in the afternoon. I stayed at home at night, I must do more cleaning at home because Mother has so much to do. I tell her I'll have the parlour to clean all to myself, she says that will just suit her. I think G. is a long while before he comes in for his tune book.

Saturday January 20th

Had a walk with Mother and Father in the afternoon. Father said G. was not coming in this afternoon to mend the spout, so I should think he is coming to do it sometime. There is always something turning up for him to come to our house. At night I called for Elly and we went to the Museum Lecture Room, "The Transit of Venus" by Mr Tangent with diagrams. They were very good, so was the lecture. I felt determined to be lively tonight and I succeeded for a little time. Elly gave me some poetry of her own composing this morning.

Sunday January 21st

I have offended my Father this morning, always up to something. I went to school this afternoon and had a walk on the cemetery after. I went to church at night. Mr Odell* preached a very good sermon from the 8th chapter of St. John 34. Elly did not meet me again, waited twenty min. for her, then I had to go alone as usual. I am never right for long together.

Monday January 22nd

I had a half day's holiday this morning, did some machining for Mother, she ought to pay me for it, I tell her. I went to work till about six o'clock, Elly could not go with me to the Lecture tonight, she said it would perhaps be better for me if she did not go. G. found a place for me, I did hear so well where I sat, but it sent him at the back. He came home with me at night. How happy I am, for I am in love, there is a secret I must not let anyone see. The lecture was by Rev. N.H. Dallinger - "An Hour with the Modern Microscope".

Tuesday January 23rd

I managed to stay at work until three o'clock today, I was talking all morning to Elly of course. In the afternoon, it was her turn, she was telling me about Tom and Addy Measures, what a day of adventures, wonders will never cease. At night I went to a sewing class at St. Margaret's School Room, I like it very much. I am beginning to know a lot of the girls, we had time for a chat, and afterwards Mrs Clayton read to us a book titled "Without a Character", then we had coffee and buns, after that we did some more work, the class broke up about nine o'clock.

Wednesday January 24th

Of course, Elly and I could not go many days without a fight, so we had a good one this afternoon, I felt quite hot for some time afterwards. At night I went to the Police Band Concert with Father and Mother, I enjoyed the concert very much indeed. But of course it rained as I went out with Father, and it was so miserable to sit in our damp clothes all night. Miss Roberts, Miss Woodhatch, Mr Dalzeth and Dr Johnson sang, and the band played at intervals.

Thursday January 25th

Elly and I had another half day's holiday so we went to the Town Museum for an hour or so, afterwards we had a walk on the Racecourse. At night I went to a Conversazione held at the Liberal Club*, Miss K. Staples was there with her sister, I enjoyed myself very much. There was a "Galvanic Battery" there, Mr Gordon and Mr Savage would have me go and try it. Oh, it did make my arms tingle but I did not shout, I did fall down when I was coming home, the wind blew and it rained so hard.

Friday January 26th

Grandfather had a day out, but he came home at night. I feel that dull and miserable tonight, I can't be cheerful for long together. Many other people seem to be happier on less hope than I have. What a thankless girl I must be, never satisfied, always craving for more. I wish I did not know what love is, it causes me a great deal of sorrow.

Saturday January 27th

I heard such a piece of news this morning, G. has said he liked me! The idea of such a thing. In the afternoon Annie Baker came down for a wonder, I was surprised. Elly came down about six o'clock, we did have some fun then. The three of us went to hear a lecture by Mr Rowlett on "Silk Culture and its Manufacture", we afterwards went to the Granby*, it's the first time I have been in that place. I do feel so very happy and jolly tonight, but I am afraid it will not last for long.

Sunday January 28th

I went to school this afternoon, there was a children's service afterwards, Mr Clayton was talking to the children on Temperance. At night Mr Clayton preached a very good sermon about the flood, I was interested in it, Genesis 6 Chapter 1 to 17 and part of the 18th verses. I think if G. liked he could make it convenient to come in more often, I so very seldom see him now.

Monday January 29th

I wish there was more space to write down all I do on Sundays, there's not nearly so much room and I have more to write. I did not see Elly again yesterday, it rained so at night. I had to take Father's Club Note between six and seven o'clock, G. made it convenient to come in tonight for about two hours. He brought some more music for me to practise, he keeps me going with new songs. He let me fall over singing, asked me to sing again, I said I could not. He heard Elly and me singing on that Saturday night, he knew I was helping her, because he said Elly had not two voices.

Tuesday January 30th

Father sent in for me to go into the Factory* at five o'clock, I spoke to A. Measures, she says she is better, how Father does tease her. He wanted me to take some money to the Bank. I went to school at night and enjoyed myself very much on the whole. I am beginning to know most of the girls now. Father was in such a good humour when he came home tonight I feel so happy and contented, how long will it last?

Wednesday January 31st

I have had the headache today, it must be through romping about so last night at the school. I broke a jug this morning as soon as I got up. L. Small came down tonight, we had a walk as far as the Oadby Road. We were coming down Belgrave Gate and met Elly, we did not stop talking long to her. I have misbehaved myself this teatime and spoken cross to Mother. I felt so sorry after I had said it, but the tea was not ready and my head ached so bad.

February

Thursday February 1st

I came home at half past four this afternoon, a short time afterwards Mother came walking home with my ulster* on, I did feel vexed at her wearing my clothes like that. I was practising when Father came home, he did discourage me, he said if any one was listening they would not think I had been learning for six years. Miss Cooper and Mr Dale spent the evening with us and we had a rare bit of fun over airing the clothes, Mother would keep talking about the drawers.

Friday February 2nd

I suppose G. and Mr Cross are going to save me a place at the Temperance Hall on Monday night, how nice that will be. It has made me feel quite dull today through seeing how Eliza is cared for by Arthur. I feel quite a "lone lorn creature", I am sure I ought not to be because I have heard a bit of good news today. Somebody says I am young and he wants to be free a little longer.

Saturday February 3rd

Miss A. Freeman wants a photo of mine, I tell her I will give her one if she will give me one of hers. While I am writing this I expect G. any minute, he is going to bring Father's watch back if it is done, but perhaps he will not come. He did not turn up, I did not expect he would. I went to hear a lecture by the Rev. Beresford Robinson on "Switzerland Dwellings in Prehistoric Times", Elly went with me. I did feel vexed, Mother wanted me to stay at home, I am glad I did not. G. is going to keep the watch a little while to regulate it, I think that's the reason he did not come.

Sunday February 4th

I had a walk with father to Mr Gordon's garden in the morning, in the afternoon I went to school. Mrs Clayton did talk nice to us on CHARITY. I met Lily and we had a walk on the park, we had tea at our house, and she went to church with me at night. I did not see Elly all day, so Lily and I had a walk at night.

Monday February 5th

I had half a day's holiday, went out with Mother in the afternoon, she bought me some scraps, Elly says what a good Mother. At night I went to the Temperance Hall with Elly, saw George, he had not a seat for himself, so he could not save us one, but we got on the back seat behind a post (E. and I) in the body of the hall. The lecture was by Mr Carpenter on the "Dynamo Machine and Electric Light", it was a very good lecture and lecturer. I thought G. was not coming to us tonight, but he caught us and brought me as far as home, we left Elly at the Clock Tower.

Tuesday February 6th

We had a holiday again, I don't know what we shall do if the trade does not stir. Elly came down to our house and we had a game at battledore and shuttlecock*, we did have some fun, she stayed to tea. I went to St. Margaret's local gathering, I enjoyed myself very well on the whole. We had games and dancing, one young fellow asked me to dance and I would not, just like me, I was afraid. I tell Mother and Father I shall have to learn, they do not agree with me at all about that, perhaps I am as well without it.

Wednesday February 7th

I went to Lily's, and we had such a delightful walk at night, we were quite chatty all the night. Lily says she expects I shall soon be engaged, I tell her she need not fear about that. We were talking about religion, she believes in GOD. I tell her she has not had her faith shaken as I have at home, but I think I have more faith lately, I hope I shall have more yet.

Thursday February 8th

I spent the evening at Miss E. Cooper's, we had a pleasant chat about work and such like. Mother says I am always out, I tell her I mean to go out more, I am the biggest soft to stay at home so much. I feel so contented just now, Father was so nice when he came home tonight he seemed quite lovable. I had to fetch the ale again, it is so cold to turn out these winter nights, when I am just getting warm.

Friday February 9th

Elly and I had to come home about ten o'clock this morning, so we had a walk on the Park, it was nice, the sun shone brightly, there are a lot of snowdrops, I should have liked a bunch. Two or three people tell me I look bad this week, I don't know how it is I am sure, I don't feel bad, but I feel dreadfully tired, perhaps it is the weather for it is so unsettled, fine one five minutes and wet the other.

Saturday February 10th

Mother saw G. this dinner time, he says he shall bring the prop sometime, I hope it will be on Monday night. I cannot get out this afternoon because it rains so fast. Elly did not call for me tonight as she said she would, so I went to the Museum Building alone. I would not have missed the lecture for ever so much, it was by H.W. Roberts Esq. on "Some of Nature's Laws of Beauty applied to our dresses and trimmings".

Sunday February 11th

G. brought Father's watch this morning, I was surprised and ashamed because I looked so untidy, he did drop on us. I went to Christ's Church* with Lily Small in the afternoon, and to their home to tea. I went to Church again at night with her and had a walk with Lily at night.

Monday February 12th

Father says George is coming tonight, I had half a day's holiday, had tea at Mrs Biggs. Elly asked me to play when I got there, so I did. It does seem strange to play on a harmonium with being used to a piano, I came home about half past six o'clock. G. came in at seven, when he had mended the prop he wanted to have a tune for a few minutes. He did not seem so shy and quiet as he usually is. He showed me a puzzle, I could not find it out because I felt so confused. Oh we got on proper tonight, he is going to bring some more of his songs, I shan't know how to face him the next time he comes in.

Tuesday February 13th

It don't appear to me as he wants to be free much longer or he would not act as he does. I think I was a bit soft to allow it but what was I to do? I did not go out tonight, I did not feel as though I wanted to so I did my ironing and made some pancakes, the stove does cook them to perfection. I do not feel like Ada Jackson today, I think I must be in dreamland. If anybody sees this diary they would think I am a silly girl, but I need not bother about that as I keep my desk locked up.

Wednesday February 14th

Mother had a valentine today, they judge me of sending it, they won't believe me when I say I did not. I suppose G. had an ugly one too. I wonder who sent it. Miss L. Small spent the evening with us, she can talk when she likes, but she is not always in the humour to talk. I did not have a valentine but I am not disappointed as I did not expect one, I have still got the glamour of love over my eyes.

Thursday February 15th

I had another half day's holiday this afternoon, I am ashamed of the money I earn, I do not know whatever I shall do if we do not get busier soon. I stayed at home and did some crocheting and netting, Mother says I can have those long curtains when I have finished them if ever I should want them, if not she shall have them. G. told Father he should bring those songs in sometime next week, and he told Father he had been trying to play on our piano. I don't suppose he would tell him about the puzzle, he judged Father of sending him that ugly valentine.

Friday February 16th

My Embroidery Machine came back, it does work so nice, I am glad it had to go to London. I managed to stay at work till five o'clock today for a wonder. Father gave me a new penny last night, for luck, he says. I shall keep it at any rate. I told Elly how happy I felt this morning, she says I may well because "somebody" is coming in tomorrow. Perhaps he will not stay long for there is not much work for him to do this time, well perhaps I shall see him for a few minutes.

Saturday February 17th

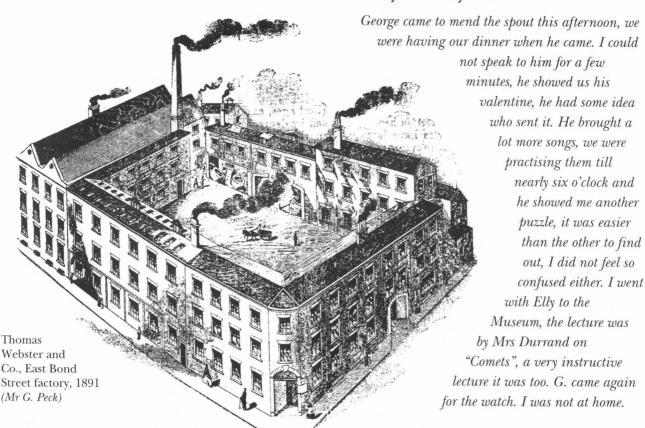

Thomas Webster and Co., East Bond Street factory, 1891 (Mr G. Peck)

George came to mend the spout this afternoon, we were having our dinner when he came. I could not speak to him for a few minutes, he showed us his valentine, he had some idea who sent it. He brought a lot more songs, we were practising them till nearly six o'clock and he showed me another puzzle, it was easier than the other to find out, I did not feel so confused either. I went with Elly to the Museum, the lecture was by Mrs Durrand on "Comets", a very instructive lecture it was too. G. came again for the watch. I was not at home.

Sunday February 18th

I went to school in the afternoon, Elly promised to meet me after, but she did not turn up. I went to church at night, Mr Lewis preached from the 1st Kings 18th chapter 21st verse, it was a very good sermon for him, I went a walk with Elly afterwards.

Monday February 19th

Father broke the glass of my watch last night through trying to close the dome. G. fastened it right on Saturday night. No work again this morning, I have been practising those songs. At night I went to the Temperance Hall with Elly to hear a lecture by Doctor Carpenter on "The Voyage of the Challenger". I could not hear well and I felt so dull because I didn't see anybody and I had to come home alone. I wonder whether he did it on purpose to slip me, Elly would not hear anything of the sort, I am a nasty tempered girl tonight Mother says.

Tuesday February 20th

Elly says I have not come to work in such high spirits this morning as I did last Tuesday. G. told Father, as he did not see me he went up the back gallery. He came for my watch tonight, he is going to have it mended for me. I say he is quite a watch agent. He asked me how I liked the lecture, he knows about Mr. Beck's wedding but he has not said anything yet. Annie has told Elly she wants me to go as well, I am surprised, I never thought as we should be such friends as we are, I went to the sewing class tonight.

Wednesday February 21st

Father brought my watch home at dinnertime and he says George is coming in tonight for a newspaper to send home. Well he came, he did not seem well I thought, he was not going to ask me to play but he did at last, he said he did not feel in the humour for singing. I do not know what to make of him, he keeps coming in but he never tells me when he is coming, he would not keep so silent if he was in love as much as I am. I am the biggest soft, I don't feel very happy tonight.

Thursday February 22nd

Elly says I must not expect things to run smooth every time, she has experienced more than I have so she ought to know. Miss A. Freeman gave me her photo this afternoon and she invited me to go and see her a week next Sunday if Elly and I can find the house. G. said last night that they were going to be married. I suppose he has known for a week or two, but he did not say anything to me.

Friday February 23rd

Elly and I went to buy Miss A. Freeman a present. Each of us gave her one, she was very pleased with them, I gave her half a dozen tumblers, she kissed me when she received them. My Grandfather is making another bother, he says he is going this time, I only hope it will come true, for he has said so many times that he is going to leave us.

Saturday February 24th

I called for Elly this afternoon and had to wait for her half an hour, I bought my round hat. When we came out of Wardles* we saw Annie Baker and Mrs. Twigger, Annie does look bad. George brought me "The Boy's Own Paper", he did not come in because he was in a hurry. Afterwards I went with Elly to the Museum, the lecture was by Mr. Simpson on "As You Like It" one of Shakespeare's plays. It was very good too.

Sunday February 25th

Mother and Father went out this morning and left me at home, I do like it for a change. George did not bring the watch, I should think it was not done. I went to church this afternoon and I had tea at Mrs. Biggs, Elly and I went down the park, then I left her and went to church, Mr. Odell preached a very good sermon, I like to hear him preach, I met Elly at night, we went for a walk.

Monday February 26th

I have trimmed my round hat tonight. I hope it will suit me, Father says it will do. I went to Annie Baker's about nine o'clock, she had gone out for a walk with John, but I saw her before I came away. It does not do me any good to see them together, because I think of myself all alone. I think George might have come in tonight, he has made it convenient to see me so many Monday nights, but perhaps he is getting tired of coming in, perhaps he doesn't think I am a nice girl now. Well, I wish he would make up his mind to do either one thing or the other. I am getting tired of this game.

Tuesday February 27th

Grandfather went to the Union* last night, it does sound well, I hope he will stop now. I went to the school tonight for the last time, Mrs. Clayton has broken the class up for this season, because there are such a few go. They will have a tea at Easter, Bella asked me if I should go, I think it is likely I shall, she will let me know when it is, I mean the day. I do feel dull and nasty tempered, I am never right for long together, talk about me reforming, it doesn't seem possible.

Wednesday February 28th

Elly called me a Mully Grubs* this morning, she says she does think I am rebellious, I feel out with myself and everyone about me. I am not a gentle girl as Mrs. Clayton talks about, I am a hard hearted one. Father asked me to go to Emery's*, of course, I had to shew my temper over it. Oh dear it will be the ruin of me. I let everybody see when a certain thing does not please me. I visited Miss Small at night she has been ill, so I stayed there about two hours. We had quite a pleasant chat about the Gilchrist Science Lectures, they asked me to stay to supper, but I did not.

March

Ada's mother, Mary Ann Jackson

Thursday March 1st

Elly and I did not go to see Miss A. Freeman married, because we had an invitation to go to Evington*, I was sorry we could not go, but if we had we would not have had a holiday this afternoon. Well, we went to Evington I was introduced to the Miss Coles I liked the oldest best, the young one seemed so quiet, I enjoyed myself very well on the whole. Mother did make me vexed, she knows something about G. and she would not tell me because I would not tell her all about A. Freeman's wedding. I had promised not to tell and I was not going to break my promise, never mind, I will be one in with her.

Friday March 2nd

Annie Baker came down last night, what a wonder, she showed me how to do a crochet pattern for edging. Father told me this morning he would take me to see "Patience"* next Wednesday night. Mother told me G. was going, I think that is what she knew last Thursday afternoon and she would not tell me. They are going on with me today about my nasty temper, they would be irritable if they had as much as I have got to put up with, but I will try to be nicer, I must appear very disagreeable.

Saturday March 3rd

Elly and I had a walk down the park this afternoon, then we went shopping. While we were gone George brought the watch, I did feel vexed, I was out, but perhaps its all for the best. We went to hear a lecture by Mr. Firth on "King John and the Magna Carta".

Elly and I did not get on at all well tonight, we don't seem to give in to each other as we ought to. I met H. Staples, Elly went walking on and she lost me for a little while, I did feel vexed at her. Kate says my round hat does suit me so should think it will do.

Sunday March 4th

I went to Belgrave Church with Miss L. Small this morning and to school in the afternoon. Elly and I went to Mrs. Beck's for tea, we were introduced to Mr. A. Beck. We all went to St. Matthew's Church* at night, I did not see anything of George there. Mr. A. Beck seemed to look after Elly very well, I could see how the wind blew, I left them at the top of Church Gate.

Monday March 5th

Elly has got a tale to tell me this morning, she is going to see Mr Beck tonight, so I shall have to go to the lecture alone, "poor lone lorn" Ada, well I shall go. We have started on 7 o'clock time at last. The lecture was by Dr. P. Martin Duncan on "The Great Fossil Mammals and Birds and their Teaching". I came marching home alone till George caught me in Gallowtree Gate and he came home with me. He sang a few songs, I could not play a bit nice, did feel ashamed of myself, he asked me if I was going to see "Patience", I think he is going.

Tuesday March 6th

Both Elly and I had got our tongues in use this morning, we had plenty to tell each other. I feel sure I have lost her now, what ever shall I do. I shall have the pleasure of roaming about alone, I shall soon get tired of that. I have sent A. Baker a birthday card for she is two and twenty tomorrow, that will shew her that I have not forgotten her altogether. I have not been out tonight, I told Mother about Elly tonight, she does think it is strange and she hopes they will keep together, we are a happy pair today.

Wednesday March 7th

I went with Father to see "Patience", George caught us up in Silver Street*, so we all went in together. He thinks it is a very lively piece, I thought he was rather quiet, we stayed to see the other piece "Mock Turtles", it was a silly lot, George said he thought it

Royal Opera House, Silver Street, 1877
(From Read R., Modern Leicester 1881)

was true, he brought me home. I wonder how it is he won't come down Church Gate. Father and Mr. Dove went before us, it was eleven o'clock when I got home, I don't know how I feel.

Thursday March 8th

I suppose Miss K. Staples saw me last night with some young fellow and she wondered who it was, no doubt Kate would like to know but I shall not tell her. It would not take much to make me weep this morning, I can't think what has come over me, perhaps it is through Elly's affair happening so quickly. I saw G. at seven o'clock he bid me goodnight. I am staying at home tonight, Elly said she might come down but I don't think she will now it is too late. Oh it is cold today.

Friday March 9th

Elly had a long tale to tell me this morning, she is happy this day and I am so miserable, my hope is fading fast. I told Father about Elly this dinnertime, he said such unreasonable things that I felt quite hurt, my mother said it is not any use taking notice of him but I can't help it. He says I am better as I am because I have got a comfortable home, he does not consider how lonely I feel and perhaps he has not tasted love, I have nearly cried so many times today. Oh what shall I do.

Saturday March 10th

I went shopping with Elly this afternoon, she called at our house after, then we went to Mrs Biggs, I had supper there. Elly left me there, she went to meet her young fellow. I afterwards went to the lecture by Montague Brown Esq. on "Spain and How the Great Bustards in the Museum were Obtained". It is the last of the season, where shall I go now, I don't know. I had a jolly good cry tonight, perhaps I shall feel better now, everything seems to be going wrong with me these last few days. Father cross, Mother unsympathetic, George quiet, Elly happy, Ada dull and nasty tempered.

Sunday March 11th

I do feel dull this morning, Mother says I am silly to show it, I went to school this afternoon, Mrs Clayton asked me about confirmation again, I don't know what to do about it, she said I was to think about it. Miss Small came down to tea and she went to church with me, Mr Clayton preached on Confirmation, we had a walk.

Monday March 12th

I went to the lecture tonight, Lily sat behind me, Mr Duncan's "The Evidence of The Antiquity of Man". Science does puzzle me, and I do feel ignorant after I have been to those lectures. Lily and I caught G. he was walking so slow, he came home with me and we stood talking for sometime. I was telling him about grandfather, he don't say much about it. I am not so happy as I ought to be, I wonder what is the matter with me. He has got one letter box ready to bring in so he tells me. All the people seem so happy they don't seem to think of ADA, I introduced Miss Small to G.

Tuesday March 13th

I do feel bad today in health and spirits, I had to open my mind after tea to Elly about Saturday, I meant to keep it to myself but I could not as usual. I feel all the better for it, though I do feel I am a blob. Elly says she will come down with me straight from work and she did, we came marching in and George was here I was surprised. He came to see about some work, he did not stay to sing. Elly stayed till ten o'clock, we had a bit of fun, I do feel happier and I will try to keep so.

Wednesday March 14th

Elly is away from work today, I am quiet, that stops my tongue altogether but I do more work. Lily came down tonight, she asked me if I was going to be confirmed, I don't think I shall this year for I don't feel fit for it. We went to the Library* and then had a walk. Lily likes G. tho' she has seen so little of him, she likes his style of shaking hands, he seems to have a firm grip, if I may so explain myself, and she had an idea he was taller than he is. I am rather happy in a calm sort of way.

Thursday March 15th

I feel so unsettled about this confirmation affair, one minute I think I will be confirmed and another I think I am not fit, I wonder how it will end. I met George at seven o'clock, I think he might stop and speak to me. There can't be much friendship passing each other in the street like that, I did not take it hard. I suppose he is going home at Easter*, there is another proof that he does not mean anything, another unhappy holiday for me, it has quite cast me down. I went to a service at the Church tonight, Mr. Clayton spoke on Holy Communion.

Friday March 16th

I hardly know what to write down today, I am in very low spirits. It is Lucy Cooper's* birthday today, I have given her a good lecture on her behaviour at home and advised her to be a better girl at home, she is going to try tomorrow. Mr Cross told George before Father that he was as good as a Father to him, George laughed, he seems a man of few words.

Saturday March 17th

I went out with Father and Mother this afternoon, Father has bought a beautiful Birthday card and Mother has bought a Hair Brush and a card for me. I ought to be a good girl but I am not. I called to see Annie Baker and stayed a long time, Mother and I went shopping, she is a cure to go out with. I trimmed a bonnet for her so I did not go out again, how lonely I feel, I had to weep when I got in bed, I remember twelve months ago today, I was in a rage over somebody.

Sunday March 18th

I went to the garden with father this morning and school this afternoon. I went on the

cemetery after, and had a walk with Father and Mother on the park after tea. Church
at night, Mr Clayton spoke on "Christ the Sacrifice".

Monday March 19th

I am twenty today, how old I am getting and the trouble I have will soon turn me grey,
I had a card from A. Baker this morning, it is such a nice one. Elly has come back to
work this morning, of course we have began talking as usual. She does seem happy, I
think that makes me feel more miserable. There was a nice present waiting for me when
I got home for dinner, it was a flower stand from L. Small. I met George at seven
o'clock, he stopped and spoke to me, he might have known what I written down here a
few days ago. He say's he thinks of going home this Easter and he shall come in some
night this week.

Tuesday March 20th

Elly gave me such a nice present this afternoon, a book and card. I tell her I have got a
bit more paper as she was teasing me yesterday about my bits of paper for presents, she
put hers in such a sweet place too, I had to go hunting for it. I went to the Swiss Choir
with Miss Ross tonight in the Cook's Memorial Hall*, I think it is a nice place and
the Swiss Choir have some tidy singers.

Wednesday March 21st

I was rather disappointed at seven o'clock as I found out that George was not here, it
made me nasty tempered, but perhaps he will come tomorrow.I called at Lily's to thank
her for my present, she was not at home. I did not stay for long, then I went up to
Annie's to thank her. Mrs Baker invited me to go on Sunday, I said I would see. Elly
has written my name in the book she has given to me. I asked her to do it, she said she
liked me for it because she thought I appreciated it.

Thursday March 22nd

George brought a chair to our house this dinnertime, I met him with it, he called in for
it tonight, it belonged to Mr. Tebbut, he kept his promise, it is a good thing he did. He
wished me "Many Happy Returns of the Day", he did not know it was my Birthday on

Monday, he did not stay long because he was going to Church. He said perhaps he would come in on Tuesday night. He tells me when he is coming in now. I feel ever so much happier and contented now, but I wish it was Tuesday, he would think I am a fool if he knew all my thoughts.

Good Friday March 23rd

I called to see Lily this morning and to thank her for that present, I asked her to come to tea this afternoon. She called for me and we had a walk on the Oadby Road, then we had tea at our house. We did not go out at night, I have enjoyed myself in a quiet sort of way, another day less to wait till Tuesday. Lily asked me to see her on Saturday, I told her about Elly, she was surprised.

Saturday March 24th

I went to work this morning it was so cold, I am glad we went for all that, it passed some of the time away. I called for Lily and went up to the Station with her to meet Mrs. Dent. It was very unfortunate, Mrs. Dent had lost her purse and could not make anything about it. We had to stop for her about an hour, well we got back again and had some tea afterwards. We had a game of cards, we were all mades Donkeys*, it was late when I got home.

Easter Sunday March 25th

It was my turn to stay at home this morning, I went to school this afternoon, it was the children's service too. I had tea at Mrs Small's and went with Lily to St. George's Church*, the singing was grand, we could not go a walk, it rained so.

Easter Monday March 26th

I do hope G. will stop tomorrow afternoon, he expects to come to work but the place will be closed. I am still at home cooking this morning. I expected Father would take Mother and I out this afternoon but I soon found my mistake out, he went marching out alone, I did feel hurt, I nearly cried over my dinner, I had to go upstairs and have it out, I felt better after. I had a walk with Mother this afternoon, it snowed nearly all the time we were out. We went home and had tea, that is the full programme for today for we did not go out again.

Tuesday March 27th

Father wanted me to go out with him this morning but I would not go as I thought Elly was coming, she did not turn up so I went out alone to the Bank and shop window viewing. I stopped at home in the afternoon with Mother, George came in about six o'clock, he kept to his promise. Father stayed at home a little longer than usual, we had quite a pleasant chat. George wanted to have a tune so we went in the parlour, he asked me if I should take cold. He stayed for supper, I shewn him my Birthday Cards and that book Elly given to me! he said they were very nice. It was nearly eleven o'clock before he went away. Oh how I love him, he was quite affectionate, I wish he would say something.

Wednesday March 28th

It was a restless night for me last night. We started to work this morning, I do feel idle, Elly and I had such a lot to talk about, I mean the holidays. We left off at five o'clock, I went to tell Father tea was ready and George was in the winding room, I did feel confused, he seemed to be laughing a great deal. Mrs Moore was here to tea, she shewn me how to do that crochet pattern, afterwards I called to see Lily Small, I do feel so happy today, the long wished for day has passed with all its pleasures (Tuesday).

Thursday March 29th

I have been thinking about Tuesday night, I don't think the right thing is going on as he has not said anything to me yet, but what am I to do, it is not in my place to mention it. When I got home tonight Mother said she thought George was coming to bring the prop. She wanted to go to a concert, I am glad she did. George came, he brought another puzzle and shown it to me when we were in the parlour. It was nearly eleven o'clock before he went away again, he met Father against the door.

Friday March 30th

Mother does seem ill today, she had to go to bed this afternoon, so I had the pleasure of doing the cleaning at night, it did tire me with not being used to it. Father asked me if

I was not well, I told him I was tired, I suppose G. was working till eight o'clock. He did not call in, perhaps he has had enough of me, I don't know what to make of him.

Saturday March 31st

Mother seems a deal better today, I had a lot to do this afternoon. I thought G. would have come this afternoon to do our letter box but he had to go round with the club money. I went out for a few errands this afternoon and I met Annie Baker, she went with me to buy a bracelet for Elly, but she did not know who it was for. I did not go out again it has made me feel tired what with cleaning and running errands.

April

Ada's father, John Thomas Jackson

Sunday April 1st

I stayed at home this morning, although it was my turn to go out. Father wanted me to go with him but I did not go. He told G. I should go the next time he asked me, he told a fib. I was at school in the afternoon, had a walk afterwards with Mother and Father down the park and I went to church at night I came straight home afterwards.

Monday April 2nd

Mother does not seem much better this morning, I hope she soon will be. I have finished reading "Pomeroy Abbey", I do think it is a nice tale. I brought Mother some biscuits home tonight, she did seem pleased with them. George was here when I got home, he was in the parlour, Father told me to light the gas. Mrs Moore came in while he was in, but stayed for all that, he sang some songs while I played for him, I did not feel in the humour for playing. It was getting on for eleven again. Before he went away he said he should be as late as usual and he told me my hair was rough.

Tuesday April 3rd

Elly and I have been gabbing again this morning, we try to keep silent for a little while, it is a struggle, we managed it for about half an hour. This afternoon I was at Mrs Biggs, we had quite a pleasant talk. While Miss Ross and Mr Biggs was out a Mrs Shipley came while I was there, she was a cheeky woman, she had the impudence to take my crocheting out of my hands and try to do it herself but she could not manage it and I did not feel inclined to tell her how it was done after that.

Wednesday April 4th

I do feel sorry for Eliza because Arthur has been bad again, she told me about it after tea, but I think it was a very slight attack. Lily came down for me tonight, we had a walk on the Oadby Road, she was telling me about "MACBETH", she went to see it on Friday night at the Opera House. She said she thought I looked bad, that is about half a dozen times this week I have been told that, it will make me bad soon if people keep telling me that. She wanted to know if I was in love, I told her I was in love with the pump if there was any love at all.

Thursday April 5th

Mother and I would like George to come to tea on Sunday but I suppose there will be something to prevent it. I suppose he would like to come in and do the rest of the work, he is working till eight o'clock at nights and he has the club money to take round on Saturday afternoons. But they say where there's a will there's a way. I should like to tell him so. I expected Eliza Cooper down tonight, she did not come, Mother spoke to G. as he passed by our house.

Friday April 6th

I went to hear a lecture on Mendelssohn, it was a sort of concert as well. Miss Deacon presided at the piano and a Miss Dent played splendidly, I went with Miss E. Cooper and L. Cooper, we all enjoyed it very much indeed. It does make me feel small at playing when I hear such good musicians as there was at Gallowtree Gate Chapel*. Mr. Baines given the lecture, he is the organist, but his business calls him to Manchester.

Saturday April 7th

I don't think George will come, Mother could not see him to ask him, my castle has fallen once more, I wonder how many more times I shall have to build, I am tired of this work altogether. Of course I stayed at home this afternoon all for nothing, I am the greatest donkey. I went out with Mother tonight for a little while and then I lost her, she called up at Mrs Baker's, A. Collier was there she wants me to go over sometime.

Sunday April 8th

I had a walk on the Cemetery this morning alone, there were some beautiful wreaths on the late Mr. Jessop's grave. Mrs Clayton's class went to Canning Place School Room* to hear a service of songs, Elly came to tea when we we got to our house. Mother and Father had gone down the Park, they met George, they brought him to tea, it was a pleasant surprise to me, he went to his own church at night and we went to ours, Elly left us to go to chapel.

Monday April 9th

Elly and I did not forget to talk this morning, I feel so very happy, George is coming to do the letter box tonight. It seems so much nicer to know when he is coming in the next time, well he came and he talked but he did not ask me to play, that was a disappointment, life is not all sunshine. He shown me a letter his sister had sent him, she seems fond of him I think. She wants him to go to London, he says if he goes at all it will be at Whitsuntide. Of course that was a damper, I wish I knew the consequence of it all.

Tuesday April 10th

Poor Elly was down in the dumps this morning as well as me, I thought she would be ever so happy. The chapel question has come on board and she doesn't know how it will end, we have been trying to cheer each other up. I feel in a don't care mood, perhaps I shall see the good of all these troubles sometime. I do feel idle this afternoon, I believe I made Elly idle as well; we have been fighting till we both feel all aglow. Kate Staples says I do look wicked with my eyes when I like, I did not know that, I think George is coming in tonight.

Wednesday April 11th

George ought to have mended the Dolly Pegs, but as mother was washing they were wet, so he came in to look at them, it did amuse me. He asked me to have a tune, I just felt in the humour for playing so we got along very well. He little thinks I write down so much about him, he would think I was soft if he did. He passed by on Tuesday night because he told me about hearing me play. Elly thinks he makes himself at home, I am very glad he does, I like him all the better for it. Oh I am so contented and happy considering things.

Thursday April 12th

Miss E. Cooper spent the evening with us, we had quite a pleasant chat, it did seem a change, for I do not have time to say much to her. She told me I must take care of Mother because she seems so bad lately. I can't think what is a matter with her, I hope she will not go wrong way, I must try and help her more than I do, as she helps me whenever she can, I have got a good Mother, all say so that know her. Eliza says she shall come again some time, I tell her she will have to ask me first, she says she shalln't.

Friday April 13th

I told Elly today how happy I felt, I was singing nearly all day, I am glad I can content myself, she thinks so too. I thought I might see George pass at eight o'clock but I did not, my spirits did go down then. Perhaps I have got to wait ever such a long time before I see him again and I do want to see him so bad, I wonder where he puts himself Saturdays and Sundays. How much longer am I to be tossed about in this manner, I do not know. Well, I must let things take their own course and wait patiently.

Saturday April 14th

Miss L. Cooper came down this afternoon, we had quite a pleasant afternoon with her singing and me playing. Elly and Eliza have gone to Evington with their men this afternoon, it makes me feel a "lone lorn creature". If I could only think that things will work right in the end it will be better for me. I had a walk at night alone, I saw Lily and Kate but they did not see me. Father seems dull, I should think it is his cold, I wish he was better.

Sunday April 15th

It was my turn to stay at home this morning. I went to school this afternoon and met Lily after, we had a walk on London Road, she had tea at our house, we went to

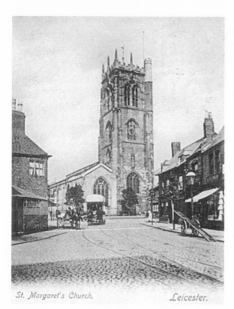

St. Margaret's Church, c.1904
(Leicester City Council)

Margaret's Church, Mr Lewis preached, Lily likes him, it was a good sermon for him. We had a walk up the road and was caught in a shower of rain.

Monday April 16th

When I got home from work tonight Mother had gone out, we wondered where she had gone to. Father told me George was coming in tonight but he was working till eight o'clock, he came before Mother got home to mend the Dolly Pegs. Of course, he asked me if we should have a tune and we had one, he seemed quite chatty and affectionate as well. If I did not care for him I think he would soon make me, it would be as nice again if I knew what his intentions were, it was half past ten again before he went away.

Tuesday April 17th

George came in for Father's watch tonight, he forgotten it last night, I would have given him a penny for his thoughts. I suppose Mrs B. does not think we shall get together yet as he does not want anybody yet awhile. He wants to be free a little longer, I think that is a nice order for me, but what am I to do? it is not in my place to propose. I wish something would happen soon so that I could know one way or the other. It is too bad tampering with me like this, I think I make too much of an idol of him, all my writing is about him and I seem to live for him alone, I know it is not the right thing.

Wednesday April 18th

I have been messed about at work today, I have had all the samples and they are a bother. He gives me such hard things to do it seems to pull me back too. I stayed at home tonight and did my ironing. If I had promised to go out somebody would have come in, as it was of course they stayed away. Father says now he thinks G. is coming in to see if he likes, Mother says, then if he does not he will go somewhere else, Father says "no" to that.

Thursday April 19th

I heard that Mr W. Blunt was dead, I can hardly think it is true it was such a shock to me, he is so young. I feel so sorry about it, what will his parents and young lady do, it will be a great trouble. I had a walk with Lily tonight, I did enjoy it, we had such a nice chat on many things. She wants me to go down on Saturday and try that duet over as we have been talking about, I should like to try it over and see what we can make of it.

Friday April 20th

At night I went out to the Sunday School Industrial Exhibition* with Miss Cooper and Mr Dale, I enjoyed it very much indeed. There were prizes for Crewel Work and Scrapbook or anything you could mention. There was a singing contest, I think it is a very good idea for it keeps some youngsters out of mischief. It seems nice to go out on Friday night, but I have to do my work on Saturday afternoon.

Saturday April 21st

I went out with Mother for a little while, afterwards I called for Lily, we had a chat about books, then we met Kate and I had a walk on the Oadby Road, what a lark we had, I laughed till they were ashamed of me, so they left me. When they came back they said something else to make me laugh so there was six of one and half a dozen of the other.

Sunday April 22nd

I went to Mrs Dove's this morning with Father, she gave me some lovely flowers, then we went to Mr Gordon's garden, I did feel tired when I got home. I went to school this afternoon and had a walk on the park after with Mother. I went to the Great Meeting Chapel* at night with Lily and had a walk after.

Monday April 23rd

I feel quiet today, it does seem a long time since I saw George, I don't know whether he will come in tonight, Father did not say. I had given him up, but he came after eight o'clock, he said he wanted a walk. We had a tune and it was after ten when he went away. *I have asked him to lend me his hymn book, I am getting bold, so is he, we do talk a lot now and seem quite used to each other, time improves us.*

Tuesday April 24th

Elly knew by my telltale face that somebody had been last night, I can't help laughing I feel so dreadfully happy. I put a lot of faith in him, perhaps too much and I shall be sorry for it someday, well, I cannot help it now. Mr W. Blunt was buried today, a lot of the girls went on to the cemetery, it does seem such a pity for him to be taken so young. Mr Odell came again last night to ask me about confirmation, I tell him I would rather let it be, but he is going to call again on Thursday.

Wednesday April 25th

Father wants me to go to the Opera House with him tonight, I don't know what to do, if I don't go, I expect I shall offend him and that will not do. Well, I have made up my mind to go, they are playing "Rip Van Winkle", it is an Opera. There is some lovemaking in it, I felt so silly a great many times. George came in to us when we had been in a little time, he was not going to have a drink when Father asked him, I like him a great deal for it.

Thursday April 26th

I expected Lily down last night, whether she came or not I do not know as Mother went out, I shall have to go and see, if she does not come tonight. I waited till eight o'clock then I went for her. I met her in Orchard St., she had not been down last night. I am glad, as I was out, we had a walk on the Oadby Road. Mrs Twigger sent the money for that cape last night, it has been done about twelve months, "Better Late Than Never", I should think that is her motto.

Friday April 27th

I stayed at home tonight and cleaned the parlour, I do feel tired. Mr Odell called again again last night to see if I would be confirmed, I did not see him but Mother told him I had decided to let it be this year. He said he was very sorry and it would not be too late to change my mind on Saturday. I know I shall not change. Mother made me so vexed tonight, she says I am not to make that marmalade after all the bother to get the recipe, I shall get the oranges and make it.

Saturday April 28th

I feel dreadfully dull this morning as though something is going to happen. I had to go to Emery's and when I was going up Belgrave Gate I met H. Collier and moved to him. I called up at Mrs Baker's, Annie was not in, I wanted to see her about a dress. Lily came down for me at about half past seven, we were going up the London Road and we met George, of course we did not stop, it was a miserable wet night. Mother says I was silly as I did not speak, just like me I was shy. People would not think we're particular friends to see us do like that.

Sunday April 29th

Father met Aunt Polly and she said Grandfather had died. It does seem a sad end to come to. I went to the Church Service this afternoon and to church at night and met Lily afterwards.

Monday April 30th

George came in last night, he copied that hymn for me, I shall think a lot of that, we had a laugh over it, he had not copied any before. Mother was washing so she had to keep going out, we were quite chatty. He did not ask me to play, it would not have been right as we had had the shutter to. Father came home while he was here, he looked rather confused when they met, I could have laughed but I dare not.

May

1 MAY TUESDAY [121-244]
St. Philip and St. James. See Hol. Table

Grandfather was brought home after tea George was here when I got home he had his tea with them he would have come to sit with us only it was club-night bother the club. Mother told him last night that Mr Odell wanted me to be confirmed he said if we all waited till we were good enough nobody would be confirmed. Elly said she would sleep with me I was very glad of that I did not like to ask her I did not think she would care to sleep as the dead was in the house

Tuesday May 1st

Grandfather was brought home after tea, George was here when I got home, he had his tea with them, he would have come to sit with us only it was a club night, bother the club. Mother told him last night that Mr Odell wanted me to be confirmed, he said if we all waited till we were good enough nobody would be confirmed. Elly said she would sleep with me, I was very glad of that, I did not like to ask her, I did not think she would care to sleep as the dead was in the house.

Wednesday May 2nd

Elly and I went to work together this morning, I had to stay away from work this afternoon to get the tea. I did not see anything of Grandfather, I am glad as I did not care to see him. George went on the cemetery, Father says he thinks G. would have liked to help carry him. I think he might have come in tonight, he can't care much or he would take more opportunities than he does, I am a good mind to roar*.

Thursday May 3rd

I had a walk with Lily tonight, it was a beautiful night, we went along the Oadby Road and we had such a pleasant chat about house-keeping. We seem to get on so well sometimes to what we do others. I don't know how it was that George did not come in, perhaps he comes in when he has "nothing else to do". I should like to tell him so, but dare not yet. I am a disappointed lover, how sorry I feel for myself, as I have not more sense.

Friday May 4th

I have been told two or three times this morning I seem in a nasty temper, it is a pity I have not more control over myself, I feel jovial and jolly for I keep singing between my temper. Mother has left her teeth at the dentist this afternoon, she did amuse me when I got home at night, she looked so peculiar, I tell her she looks as old as her Father. I laughed at her till I did not know what to do with myself, my sides ached, so I helped to do some of the cleaning tonight.

Saturday May 5th

It did snow this morning, it seems more like Christmas than near Whitsuntide, I hope it will be finer next week. I thought G. was coming in for his boots, another disappointment, the people where he lives are moving so he can't come. I called to see Annie Baker at night, she said she wanted to see me as she had something to tell me. Their furniture is going to be sold by auction and they would be turned into the street if Mrs Emerson had not offered to help them, I felt so sorry for Annie, she is in such trouble over it.

Sunday May 6th

I went on the cemetery this morning for a walk, I went to school in the afternoon and had tea at L. Small's, Miss Houghton was there too. We called at Miss Houghton's after tea then went to Christ's Church, a man was in a fit while Mr Isaacs was preaching, it startled most of the people. I had a walk with Lily on the Oadby Road, we met Elly and her young man but she did not see me.

Monday May 7th

Elly went to St. Matthew's Church last night, she saw George walk with the choir, I did feel miserable, I nearly cried two or three times and she was so happy. When I got home at night Mother said G. was coming about eight o'clock for this book, I gave him up at last because it was nearly nine when he came. I was in a stew, I felt very rebellious. He did not sing, I wonder how it was he asked me about singing again when we were in the parlour, he is not going to London but he is going to visit another sister, I wonder what he means.

Tuesday May 8th

Miss B. Cooke was telling me about Mrs Oldershaw, she has gone through an operation at Birmingham and while I was talking to her George passed, I did feel confused, I am sure she would notice me, I could not help it. I expect I shall often meet him at two o'clock, I wish I did not in a way, I feel so silly and it makes me think, but for all that I like to see him. He ought to say what he means, I don't think it seems honourable to go on as we are, I wish I could find a way of knowing.

Wednesday May 9th

Lucy Cooper is working against us, we do have some larks, we are always up to something, knocking each other on the floor fighting, it makes me very idle. I saw George again at two o'clock, I did not know how to walk or where to look when I saw him coming, he appeared something the same. I thought he did laugh, I wonder what he was laughing at, he was with Arthur Samuels, perhaps it was at him. I did not go out tonight, it is so wet.

Thursday May 10th

George told Father he would mend the window sashes down Chestnut Street. I went in the parlour to practice, when I had been a short time I thought some children had knocked at the door, I went to the door to frighten them and who should stand there but George, another pleasant surprise. He said he thought he would come then, as he would not have another chance before he went to his sister's for his holidays. I wonder if he heard me singing, he did not say anything about it, I should hardly think he did, he was talkative, I liked him ever so much.

Friday May 11th

I feel in such good humour today, we had a few games at work, George said last night he thought we had a few larks. I told him we did especially when L. Cooper was down our end of the room. I did not go out tonight, there was plenty of cleaning to do, so I helped with it, how it tires you to clean. I wish I was always in such high spirits as I am today, I think I must be in love, what a thing it is to be in love with a common place man.

Saturday May 12th

I asked Lucy Cooper to come down this afternoon to sing, she stayed till after seven o'clock. I went down to the fair* with Elly at night, we met Kate Staples and Polly Hickling, we were very quiet, it is a poor fair, it is hardly worth going down, there don't seem to be half the fun as there used to be. H. Collier was down, I saw lots of people that I knew, I wonder whether it will get to G., perhaps somebody will let him know about it.

Sunday May 13th Whit Sunday

It was my turn to stay at home this morning, I went with Mother to the Children's Flower Service this afternoon, I have not been to one before. Father and Mother and I had a walk round the park after tea, then I went to church. Mr Lewis preached, I met Lily after and we had a walk on the Oadby Road.

Last annual fair to be held in
Humberstone Gate in 1904.
(Mr B. Keymer)

Monday May 14th

I called at Mrs Baker's this morning to ask Annie about my Dress and Jacket, she will try to make them next week, I am sure I need them I feel so shabby on Sundays. H. Collier came up a while I was there, she is coming down a week on Sunday if nothing happens. I went on the park with Lily this afternoon to hear the band, she introduced me to a friend of hers Mr MacCann, he stayed the rest of the afternoon with us. We had tea at our house, then we called at Lily's, the Miss Palmers were there, we all went down the fair, we left the others and went down the fair again.

Tuesday May 15th

Miss E. Cooper came down this morning but she did not stay long as I was to see Lily, we made up our minds to go to Belvoir Castle* with the Miss Palmers and Ellen, Lily and I by the half day trip. I think we all thoroughly enjoyed ourselves, we managed to get into the Castle, that is just what I like. We saw the family portraits, Ballroom, Drawing Room etc. and we got in with strange company on the train both going and coming back. We had to wait for the train about an hour and half before we could get in one to come home. The Station Master was civil, he is an exception to the general rule, he shook hands'with some of our party and bid us goodnight.

Wednesday May 16th

I stayed at home this morning as Mother wanted to go out, so I had a walk up town after dinner. Mr and Mrs Dove came to tea, I think I should like Mrs Dove when I was more familiar with her. Elly came down to see me at night, I did not expect her, she had a lot to tell me. George came while she was here, she would not stay long when he came. He brought some wild flowers this dinnertime, they asked him to come to tea but he would not. I don't mind much, he can't think how much he makes me care for him or he would not do as he does, he gradually progresses.

Thursday May 17th

We started to work this morning, I did feel idle all day, most of us wanted a half day but we had to work till five o'clock. I met Father, I wanted to buy my dress but the shops were closed so I called to see Elly. She was disappointed Arthur could not see her as he had got a swelled face. She wanted me to stay with her but I had promised to see Elly, she had gone out when I got to their house, I met her down the fair, George was going down when it was time to come home.

Friday May 18th

I shall be glad when this week has gone, I feel so tired and idle, I have not earned much this week, Mother is going halves she says so. George came in this dinnertime to help shake a carpet, he sang before Father, I thought he seemed rather shy. Father wanted to hear "My Wandering Boy", he said I was singing it at work this morning.

He came again, Father went out and left us alone, I don't care now, I am more used to him, he went home in a hurry because we heard Father coming up the entry, it was cut off short so Mother told me.

Saturday May 19th

Annie went with me to buy my dress and jacket, when I got home George was here doing some work. Lucy Cooper came for her Temperance Book, I got her to sing, he was here at the time, he stayed till Father had gone out then he went the front way. We stood talking in the parlour for a little while, he said Taylor would be waiting for him but he said he ought to attend to business first and pleasure after. I went down the fair and met Lily and Kate, we did have a lark, I went into a laughing fit again.

Sunday May 20th

Mother has got the headache again so I shall have to stay at home again this morning. I went to school this afternoon, Miss Dunmore gave us our lesson, I don't care for her, I hope Mrs. Clayton will be back for another Sunday. I went to Christ's Church, Mr Gladstone preached, I did not care for him much, Lily and I had a walk at night.

Monday May 21st

George came in tonight to do some work of course, he is a regular attendant lately. Of course he wanted to sing, he bothered me to sing, so with a great deal of persuasion I made a noise. I can't think where I got the courage from, he did beg of me before I could, I am so afraid he will laugh at me up his sleeve as the saying is. Of course he was very affectionate when I had done as he wanted me. He said that many did not do so well when they first started; a bit of flattery. Mother and Father seem to think it will be all right now, but there will have to be something said before I think so.

Tuesday May 22nd

I had to go to Mrs Twiggers to have my dress and jacket fitted on by Annie, I walked part of the way with Kate Staples, it doesn't seem nearly so far when you have company. I think Annie and John seem fond of each other because he came up for her and she says they are getting along alright except for having a tiff now and then. I tell her that she must expect that as all lovers quarrel now and again, then make it up sweeter than ever. She very seldom says anything to me on the subject now, nor about me either.

Wednesday May 23rd

Elly went with me about a hat tonight, we went down to Havelock Street where Mrs Twigger had advised me to go but she could not trim one for three weeks, of course that was no use so we went to Gee's* after all, it will cost me a pretty penny. George was here when I got home to do some work, we had a tune after the business was done, he bothered me to sing again, I have made a start and expect I shall have to go on, we are getting quite bold and talkative. He is going to do the bookcase at last, I tell him it is wonderful, I think he means it this time. I forgot to say yesterday morning Eliza and I began our morning walk for the first time this summer, I hope it won't be the last.

Thursday May 24th

Eliza and Arthur had a bother this week, they made it up again last night. I thought he would have to send for her or he was a different Arthur Dale than I thought he was. Kate told me this morning she heard that I was engaged to a schoolmaster and different people keep asking mother if I am engaged, they seem to think and know more than I do myself. I had Lily down to see me tonight, she is going to London on Saturday to a wedding, I expect she will be away for about a week or more, I tell her she is a lucky girl.

Friday May 25th

We are getting short of work again, a few of us had to go out for an hour this afternoon. I went to Mrs Twigger's for my dress and jacket tonight, it was a great bundle, Annie came down with me. When I got home George was here, I am sure he knew what I had got, I was vexed in one way, of course I was pleased to see him here, we progressed favourably. I felt so talkative and we had a bit of fun, but I wish he would say something. It seems to me as though he is trifling with me, I should be vexed with myself if he was to go now.

Saturday May 26th

We had to come home again this morning, so I went with Elly to Mrs. Twigger's, it was a miserable wet day. I went out with Eliza in the afternoon, we called to see Elly in her new hat, Eliza thinks it don't suit her, I expect she will have to have it. I called for my hat, I do like it, they think it suits me. I expected to find George here when I got home, it was a great disappointment for nobody was at home. I must have misunderstood him for I quite thought he would come. I know he said something about bringing the watch, but I don't think he will come tonight now. Oh, how miserable I feel, that shows how I should miss him if he was never to come again.

Sunday May 27th

Happy Day! G. brought the watch this morning, Mother asked him to come to tea and he said he would. I have had a good cry this dinner time because Father has been blowing Mother up about a paltry piece of fish, I feel so sorry for her. I went to school this afternoon, Mrs Clayton was nicer than she has ever been before. Miss A. Collier came to tea, she thinks George is a nice quiet young man, I did not ask her for it, he went to his own church and we went to Margaret's.

Monday May 28th

I feel so sick and bad this morning and I have lost my appetite, I seem to be going wrong altogether, I think it must be the suspense I am in, I nearly fainted this morning. Father has not got over the fish bout yet, he had gone out when I got home tonight. He had left word with Mother that I was to go down the park to hear the band, Mother persuaded me to go, so I had a walk with her. I suppose it will be nine o'clock if George comes at all tonight. We got home earlier but no George came, no doubt he thinks I am fool enough to stand for anything. I think it is too bad of him, for he has come for so many weeks on Monday night, I very nearly cried again.

Tuesday May 29th

I met George this dinner time, I felt as tho' I could forgive him for not coming last night the moment I saw him. Mother saw him at six o'clock, he told her that he had been working last night and he was going to the club tonight, he told her Mr Cross saw us down the park, we did not see him, I wonder why he told George. I went to Eliza's to help her alter a jacket, Lucy shown me a pullover of hers that is too large for her, they are going to get me to alter that. Eliza says thay will soon make a dressmaker of me for I do something of the sort nearly every time I go. We had a bit of a lark, Lucy pushed me all my length on the floor for one thing.

Wednesday May 30th

I had a walk round the park with Father tonight, we saw some people playing Lawn Tennis, I should like to learn to play, I think it is very good exercise. I called at Mrs Small's to ask if they had a letter from Lily but she had not written, I should think she has so much pleasure to attend to, that she has not had time to write. G. has not been in yet this week, I think he might find time to come in tonight, I felt as though I would have gave anything to have found him here when I got home, well I found Mrs Moore instead, she sang a bit I did not find much pleasure in playing tonight.

Thursday May 31st

I left off work about four o'clock this afternoon, we don't seem much busier, I shall go wrong if I don't get more money soon. I called to see if Annie had come back from Belton but she had not, I want my dress altering before Sunday. I met Father and went on the Race Course to hear the Band, music seems more interesting to me now than it used to be, it must be a link to love. Somebody is so busy at work and he has the Church to attend to so that they can't take a while to come in here, I feel disgusted at everything. Father says he is working so hard to make an excuse to come in, I say he ought to come in without that sort of thing now. Father does not tell me and I say very little to him about G., I mean no more than common place things.

June

George Beecroft

Friday June 1st

We don't seem to get any busier at work, I had to come home this morning so I helped Mother with the cleaning at night, I scoured my bedroom floor, I do feel tired, I am not used to such hard work. Annie Baker came down to see about the alteration of my bodice, we sat in the parlour talking. I heard somebody stop aginst our door and I happened to turn my head, I saw the cover belonging to the letter box move then they walked away, I feel sure it was George, he must have seen Annie and he would not come in, I shall wait and see if he says anything about it.

Saturday June 2nd

I do feel in bad spirits this morning, I should like to have a good cry then perhaps I might be better. I quite thought George would have come this afternoon, trouble is coming from all quarters, it is above a week since he came, I begin to think he has forgotten me and is getting tired. I am dull, I have had a cry, I have wished I was out of this world, what a dreadful bad girl I am. Mrs Lewis told us last Sunday to put our trust in the Lord, I am not doing that or I should not be so rebellious, but I do think I am tried. I don't think G. will come tonight now, I shall have to give him up now.

Sunday June 3rd

Father went out for the day this morning, I don't like the house without him, it seems so strange. It was my turn to stay at home to get the dinner, I went to school in the afternoon, Miss Dunmore took the class. I went to Belgrave to tea, Mr Bevans was there too, he was teasing me, he said his name began with B. I think Harry and all of them know about George, I went to the IRON CHURCH* with Annie and her Mother, the text was "Be Strong", Harry did not come part of the way home with us, he left it all to Annie this time.

Monday June 4th

I suppose George tried to get in with Father's watch twice yesterday, it was in the morning and after Church at night, I am glad in one way as I was not at home at night, it would let him see I did not always stay at home. I went down to the park tonight for a little while, I got home about nine and George was here. I tried to be cool but it was no use, he seemed so very attractive, he bothered me to sing, the more he asks me the more stubborn I seem. He stayed till after Father came home, we were all talking for sometime, then Mother and Father left us in the parlour alone.

Tuesday June 5th

Eliza Cooper came down tonight for a little time, she wanted me to do her some machining, she went away just before nine o'clock. George came in soon after she had gone, he brought some of the wood belonging to the bookcase, I asked him if he was going to do anything to it, he laughed and said "No". Of course we went in the parlour, he wanted to have a few hymns as it was too late for songs, he asked me if I would learn to sing and play "It is Well", I told him I would see, I had a walk alone this morning down the park, he saw me.

Wednesday June 6th

I stayed at home and I was trying to sing "It is Well". I feel wonderfully happy, I wonder how long it will last. I ironed the collars, it seems as though I have not got anything to say today, I think it must be through neglecting you so my diary. I don't write anything for days together, it is a very bad habit to get in to.

Thursday June 7th

I met somebody this dinnertime, I don't know how to look or walk when I meet him sometimes. At night I went to hear Professor Moore's lecture, Elly went with me, she had a pleasant surprise when we had been there sometime. I saw Arthur there, of course I soon told Elly, she would hardly believe me, but I was right. She introduced me to Mr Watson, a brother in law of his, they came down Church Gate with me. I told Elly she was good, I liked him ever so much better this time I saw him. I did enjoy the lecture, I would have gone before if I had thought they would be so interesting.

Friday June 8th

George came in this dinnertime to bring some tools. We had such a lark at work this afternoon at my expense I felt as though I did not care whether I worked or not and I should have liked my tea at home. Miss Ross told me to come home once, then she brought me some work, every time she brought me the bits Elly laughed at me. G. had his tea at our house, I was at home when he came, I don't know what he will think of us for we were laughing and making fun all the night. He stayed to supper, he asked if he should go out of the front door. Father shook hands with him and told me to go to the door, I don't know what to make of that.

Saturday June 9th

I might as well of stayed at home this morning for what little work I have done, I had to come home again. George came to work again this afternoon, we have not got on so well since the other Friday night, I should think it is the work, he stayed till half past seven. He told me he has got to see his friend at eight, I can't think what keeps him from proposing, I think he must know he would be accepted. I made up a piece of poetry as I had promised Elly for a long time now, there were four verses of rubbish, I hope she will not let anybody see it.

Sunday June 10th

I went to Harvey Lane Chapel* sermon this morning, Eliza introduced me to Mr Nicholas a cousin of Arthur's, he went home and I had a walk with Eliza and Arthur. I went to school in the afternoon and had a walk with Elly afterwards, it seems like *old times again. I went to Margaret's Church again at night, then I had a walk as far as Mrs Small's, I have missed Lily tonight, they don't know when she is coming home.*

Monday June 11th

I had to come home again this morning for the day, I went out with Mother to buy a bonnet shape, George came in this dinnertime. Father told him I could help him tonight, then he asked me to fetch some glass for him. I went in the Winding room to Father, George came in while I was there. Elly came for tea, I showed her how to do Crewel work. George had his tea here, I was in the parlour with him, we had a sensible chat, he was enquiring about Elly and the church. Lily came about nine I was surprised to see her, she came home about six, she asked me to go to the post with her, I could not very well refuse. G. was at work when I got back, I did feel sorry for him he seemed so tired. Oh, how I love him, I wonder if he cares a little bit for me.

Tuesday June 12th

We are in a mess this week, we are having the house cleaned so we are topsy-turvy. I am sitting on the floor in my bedroom to write this. I managed to stay at work all day, at night I was cleaning some of the furniture. Elly stole one of my flowers last night, I said I would pay her out so I gave her a good shaking when I got to work this morning, she wondered where she was for a few minutes. We have had to get up at six o'clock these last two mornings, I felt so tired and helpless this afternoon that I was the laughing stock for Elly, she was mocking me I nearly fell asleep while I was working.

Wednesday June 13th

We had to get up at six o'clock again this morning, I should like to get up early every morning, I shall try, I don't know how long it will last. G. came in this dinnertime, he did not say what for, and he came in again at night, he hung the pictures up. We were in the parlour alone most of the time, it was such another night as that Friday, we had a bit of fun. I am getting quite used to him, it seems such a pleasure to see him here, he told me that I should go down the park on Sunday mornings. I think that was a broad hint, it was after eleven when he went away.

Thursday June 14th

I came home at five o'clock, the house cleaning has knocked Mother up so she has had to go to bed, her head aches so and she has a bad cold. I have one too, I should think it is the draught. I did a lot of cleaning tonight, there was nobody here to hinder me, it's just as though I can't get on with anything when he is here. I should like to see him for all that much wants more. We are dreadfully short of work, I do not know what I shall do for I want the money so very bad just now to get out of debt and I should like to go to London for the day when Ellen and Mrs Houghton go.

Friday June 15th

Father stayed at home again tonight, George wanted to know how much I would bet, I tell him, I shall not bet again because very likely I shall lose. George had supper with us, it seems as nice again when Father is at home. We were left in the parlour alone for a time, that makes me think Father understands the matter and I think he knows something too, or he would not act as he does, it was as pleasant a night as the other Friday, we got larking and trying to knock each other's hands, he did seem affectionate.

Saturday June 16th

I came home again this morning about twelve, Elly has had another bilious attack so she did not come to work. Somebody came again this afternoon to work, of course, we had a tune that is something new, he seemed rather quieter as far as affection goes. He asked me why I went away from him, he was trying to brush me and I sent the brush in his face, fun again. He asked if I was going to see Lily, he said that he should be done with the club about next Christmas, so I don't think he will say anything yet, he ought to explain himself I think. I called for Lily, Kate was there, the three of us had a walk, I felt very quiet, I had such a cold.

Sunday June 17th

I had a walk with Father as far as Mr Dove's and then we went to Mr Jordan's garden. When we got home there was a row, the dinner was not cooked properly, it is aggravating, but I own Father was in a temper. I went to school in the afternoon, George came to tea, we did not get on very well I think, so he asked me if I was going to Margaret's Church but he did not ask me to go to his church, I didn't feel very happy after church. I met Lily and we had a walk.

Monday June 18th

I had half a day's holiday again this afternoon and I had tea at Mrs Biggs. Miss Ross sent for Elly about four o'clock, she was vexed, I should have been if I was in her place, she was only there for an hour. We had a walk on the park after tea, I had a bit of fun of course. A little brat called us two fools, he was a naughty boy. George came about nine for a walk, he has got the toothache so bad now, I feel so sorry for him, I wish I could make it better for him. He brought a book for me to read titled "Courtship and Marriage", he said it was a strange subject and he seemed as though he could not show me the book. This is another singular event as I cannot understand, he said he should come in on Wednesday night.

Tuesday June 19th

I have begun to read that book, there is some good advice in it, I wonder if he is acting on the advice of that book, it looks a great deal like it. He came in this dinnertime to put the letter box up again, poor lad, he has still got the toothache, he saw me down the park before breakfast this morning. He said he had got to go to his club tonight, I don't understand it. I am staying at home tonight, Mother has been washing today, well I think I will practise now, I soon got tired of practising, there was nobody here to sing.

Wednesday June 20th

I am altogther disgusted with the work, I was there till four o'clock and earned scarcely anything, it is a humbug of a place. We had a bit of a lark at home, I hung Father's paper up, he was obliged to laugh. It was gone half past eight and George has not come yet. Oh if he does not come what shall I do or think. It was nine when he came, I don't care now, he had put my bedstead up. His tooth has left off aching now, he asked me if I had read any of that book, he wondered if I was reading it down the park the other morning.

Thursday June 21st

I left off about five again today, I tell them at home if it lasts much longer I shall go wrong. We had such a laugh at home when Father got home, the subject was about Mother going into the dirt hole, I met Lily tonight and as soon as we got on the Race Course I felt my drawers coming down so we had to go into Waterloo Street to fasten them up. We did not hear much music, Lily was pleased with her apron and thanked me very much for it. She saw George on Tuesday night and did not like to speak, he told me that he saw her, they were both shy at that rate.

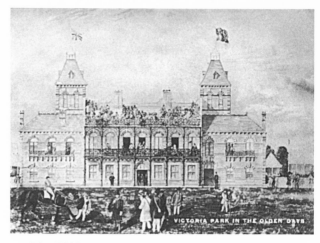

The Old Racecourse, now Victoria Park.
The Leicester Races were last held here in 1883
(Mr B. Keymer)

Friday June 22nd

It is hard work treadling but it is better than going home. George stopped and spoke to me this dinnertime, that is a bit more, it will soon be noticed if he goes on with it. I should like to know if he is coming in tonight, but I don't suppose he will. I stayed at home and helped with the cleaning. Father says he has gone to do some work for Mr

Harris and he is going tomorrow afternoon, I mean George, perhaps I shall not see
him till Monday night. It will seem a long time because I have seen so much of him
lately.

Saturday June 23rd

Elly has been giving me a lecture, she says I am so unreasonable if he does not come in
as much as usual. Her and Eliza are going to Evington this afternoon with the two
Arthurs, it makes me feel my loneliness and so dissatisfied with my lot, it generally
happens as they go when I am all alone. Father has gone to a cricket match, so Mother
and I went marketing this afternoon. Lily came down for me at night, we had a walk
as far as the Race Course and sat down, we met Kate on the London Road, she went
down with us. I do feel miserable and quiet I shall be glad when I am in bed and
asleep.

Sunday June 24th

I stayed at home this morning and Mother went out, it was the children's service this
afternoon. I went to church at night with Mother, then I met Lily and Miss Hickin, we
went up to the course, Lily said I was quiet. I could not talk, she will think it was
because there was three of us.

Monday June 25th

Elly has been lecturing me again, she thought I had come to work in one of those nasty
moods this morning, she did not feel inclined to talk to me, that shows what a nasty
thing I am sometimes. I met George this dinnertime, he stopped and spoke, he says
perhaps he shall come in tonight. I had to go of an errand for father to fetch the rents
as he had gone to Coventry on business, I got wet through, it was a thunderstorm. G.
came about nine, he wanted a tune if I was not too tired. He shown me a letter his
sister had sent him, and he is going home on Saturday, but he says he shall come
again before then.

Tuesday June 26th

Elly and I arranged to go and see Mrs Beck, we hardly thought we should get there because there was a thunderstorm, but we started soon after eight. Mrs Beck said her husband had gone to the club, she was chattering away I think she seems happy, I am very glad. I was introduced to Mr and Mrs Watts, a sister of Mrs Beck's. Annie said that Arthur was very delicate, not very good news for Elly, we did not hear much.

Wednesday June 27th

I was writing all my news down here and who should pass the window but George, I didn't think he would come down tonight, he was trying to work my machine. We said he was flowering, he asked me if Elly and I went to Mrs Beck's, of course, we went in the parlour to have a tune, he said he thought I was very strong. I told him I hoped he would enjoy himself, but he said he should come in on Friday night, the idea of such a thing, I did like him, it was a pleasant surprise to see him so soon.

Thursday June 28th

I have heard enough to set me against Arthur Beck, I feel downright sorry for Elly, I don't know what ever she would do if she knew, but she might overlook it as she is so fond of him, the beast, for he is nothing else. Lily called for me tonight, we had a walk on the course to hear the band. There seems a something between Lily and I and it appears as though we can't agree on many subjects and I can't open my mind to her because I fancy she thinks I am a silly girl.

Friday June 29th

It has been so hot today, there was hardly a breath of air, I think it's the hottest day yet. There was a thunderstorm after tea, it was very heavy. I got my cleaning done early tonight because I expected somebody, it was about half past nine when he came, I began to think he could not get, he was very chatty. I thought he did look nice, I quite admired him, he has taken some of his music home and one of my songs, he says I am to mind how I go on. I tell him to behave himself, he is coming in on Tuesday night.

Saturday June 30th

I feel so happy today, I wish I could always feel as contented and peaceful. It seems hotter than ever, it's quite unbearable but I suppose we shall have to put up with it. I *went shopping with Elly this afternoon, I have bought a new straw hat. I called for Lily, her sister Ellen seems much better now. We met Kate in Belgrave Gate, she introduced us to Miss Kemp, we all went on the course. I thought Lily seemed very quiet, she said she felt very tired, we went in the Market House*, the flowers smelt so sweet.*

July

Sunday July 1st

I stayed at home this morning, Mother is not very well again, I went to school this afternoon, afterwards I went to Mr Jordan's garden to tea with Mother and Father, Mr and Mrs Dove were there too, we went to see Mr Samuels' garden and several others. I could not get away to church, it seems so strange as I am used to it now. I had to make haste to meet Lily, then I was late. We had a walk as far as the Course, I feel so tired.

Monday July 2nd

We are having some hot weather, it seems unbearable, but I suppose we shall have to get used to it, I like winter best, well I shall have to wait for that. Lily came down for me tonight, we went down the park, we saw Father and Mr Leaver, each of us had a Passion Flower, it was the first Lily had. It is something new for me to go out on Mondays, I hope he is enjoying himself, I wish it was Tuesday, I feel rather happy on the whole.

Tuesday July 3rd

I have made up my mind to go to the vicarage to tea, Mrs Clayton asked us all on Sunday. Mary Ann Fowler and I went together, the table was set out nicely, after tea we had games, I enjoyed myself very much. When I got home George was here, of course he wanted a tune so we went in the parlour but I did not play much, we were talking. I told him it was a pity he could not stop a little longer as he might have enjoyed himself more. He said he was enjoying himself here, I said I did not know. I do like him, tonight he seems so nice and I think he looks nice too, perhaps it is that crimson tie he wears.

Wednesday July 4th

I feel stiff and tired this morning, perhaps it is through romping yesterday. Father asked George to go to Mr Jordan's garden with him tonight. I have had an idea he will call here when he leaves Father, I don't know why I should. Well! it is after nine, I had given him up so I went into the parlour to practice, I had not been there many minutes when a knock came at the door, it was him. Oh, I fell down while he was here, I thought the stool was against me and it was not. I did feel vexed yet I had to laugh, I wish he would say something instead of going on like this, it is cruel.

Thursday July 5th

We went to the Floral Entertainment at the Liberal Club*, there was a magnificent show of flowers, the concert was rather nice too. There was a lot of shaking of hands and introducing. Mr Mason said my young man was there, I said it was Father's friend. George said he must see as I did not fall down tonight, he came all the way home with me. I was rather surprised as he had no need to, Father and Mother were with me, he enjoyed himself very much indeed. I don't know when I shall see him again, he has work to do, fancy, three nights running.

Friday July 6th

We had a half a day's holiday, short of work again, so I did my cleaning and went with Lily and Kate to hear the Police Band. We did have a lark, I was ashamed when we were going up the road. Ellen asked me if I should go to London with them on Belgrave Wake Monday*, I should very much like to go if I can afford it. I told Father, he seems to think I have not the money to spare, well, I shall see. I do feel tired, I have been out such a lot this week.

Saturday July 7th

Eliza Cooper and I had a walk on the Oadby Road, it seems like olden times, she was telling me some news, I thought she would if I left it to her. She says she would like me to help her with her house linen affairs, we had quite a pleasant chat. I arrived home about six o'clock so tired and I had promised to call for Lily, I went about eight and had another walk on the Oadby Road. I was glad enough to get home, I was so tired I must stay at home more this next week and do some work.

Sunday July 8th

George brought Father's watch this morning, I had an idea he would come, something told me so. Oh I was ashamed, Mother told him I had got diarrhoea, I was vexed at her. I was at school in the afternoon and afterwards went with Father and Mother to have tea at Mrs Dove's. I managed to get to church at night, Mr Clayton preached a good sermon on "Repentance and Temptation", I put it to myself. I met Lily afterwards, we saw her friend Mr MacCann, he went home with her.

Monday July 9th

I met George this dinnertime, he said perhaps he should come in tonight, he came about half past eight, Mother had gone to hear the band. He asked me if I would teach him music, I said I would willingly, what little I knew. He was enquiring about our trip from Websters to Skegness, he seemed as if he would like to go by the half day trip. Miss Cooper and Mr Dale called around about half past nine, we did have a lark, we made some fun. Afterwards, the four of us decided to go to Skegness, Arthur and George arranged to come for the half day. I think they were both well pleased about it. I am glad they know each other, I think they would get on first class.

Tuesday July 10th

Eliza and I had a walk before breakfast, I enjoyed it very much, it is possible Eliza did too. George stopped me this dinnertime to ask me how we had arranged for Saturday but I hardly know yet. Eliza and Elly came at night, we did have a spree, while they were here Mrs Smith came, we all felt inclined to laugh when we saw her because we have such fun out of her. Elly made me scream and she frightened me, I sent her on the floor. Then Eliza started calling on me, then Elly rounded on me, I don't think she will go to the holiday on Saturday, I should like her to go but I think we should be better without her company.

Wednesday July 11th

What a bother we have had with our work this morning, we learn fresh things, then when we get used to them Miss Ross don't give us any more, I am getting on bad this week. I am staying at home tonight, it is about time I did, it seems lately I am always out or somebody is here. I have been preparing for Saturday, George seems anxious to know how we have settled, I think the four of us will go now but we don't know what may turn out between now and then. I feel so sleepy tonight, I think I shall have to go to bed before Father comes home.

Thursday July 12th

Eliza told me she met George this dinnertime at two, I saw him afterwards and wondered what made him laugh so knowingly, I see now, or I think I do. Lily came down for me tonight, we went on the course and saw Eliza and some friends. I feel quite sure Lily would have come on Saturday till I told her George and Arthur was coming by the half day trip. I am afraid she will think I did not want her as I did not press her to go, I do feel sorry. I called to see Annie Baker, they have had an alteration to their house, I think she will come to tea on Sunday and perhaps John will come.

Friday July 13th

I have scarcely done any work again this morning, I wish there was more, of course I have got some fresh work to learn again, Miss Ross says I cannot learn too much. The machine will not work on twilling, bother it, we were paid tonight, there was a confusion. It was about half past nine when George came tonight, I began to think he could not get, he said he hoped we should enjoy ourselves. There has been a heavy thunderstorm about six o'clock, George came in to borrow an umbrella, he is often trotting in, I don't care how soon it is morning, the secrets I have written down here.

Saturday July 14th

We started for Skegness* after eight o'clock this morning, we had such a lark in the train. I think it is a nice little place, we did not care to mix up with the girls because of them coming in the afternoon. Eliza and I got a good wetting, through sitting on the

70

sands too near the water, I had to wring her dress out at the bottom. Their train got in just before five, I thoroughly enjoyed myself, the time did seem to go quick, in the afternoon we went on the pier. We could not get on the steamer or a boat, I was rather disappointed. The train got in about twelve, George came home with me. Elly was here to sleep, she did make me scream for she got hold of my leg from under the table.

Sunday July 15th

I have got the diarrhoea again today and I think I have caught a cold in my eye, it does run, I managed to go to school. Elly and Arthur and George came to tea, we were playing and singing after tea of course. George went to his own church and I went to mine, they went to chapel. I met Lily after, we went on the course, Elly brought her young man in, I hardly thought he would come in, Mother says he looks quite a young man, we had a bit of music.

Monday July 16th

I met Mr T. Bevins, he asked me if I was going to Skegness with them tomorrow, I said I went on Saturday. Elly promised to come down and go out with me this morning, I can't think the reason as she did not. I went out alone, I called in Horn's shop*, they kept me such a long time it was one o'clock when I was coming home. I met G. he

71

asked me if I should be at home tonight as perhaps he should come in. I had tea at Mrs Cooper's, Eliza and I had a walk, she showed me her things she has got towards housekeeping. G. came in about eight o'clock, he had his first music lesson, I think he would soon pick up some tunes, he said he did not know when he should get in again, that seems dreadful.

Tuesday July 17th

We started to work this morning, I hope we may have more of it now. I feel rather miserable this morning, I can't think what has come over me, I wonder what fever I have got now, there is always something in this wide world of sorrow. Most of the girls have enjoyed themselves at Skegness by what they say. I am staying at home tonight, Mother and I are alone, it does seem dull. I think it is time I settled down to some work of some sort. Eliza has done a lot, I am as idle as can be, just like me. I will do more work from now, there is a resolution I hope I shall fulfil, I am dull and drowsy.

Wednesday July 18th

I have felt sleepy ever since I came back from Skegness, I should think it is the sea breeze. I am going to try and be more loving and patient and forgiving, to think more of the present and not so much of the future, I ought to be happy. Mrs Dove sent a letter to thank us for that ball, I do think that looks well of her. I do like her she is just my sort, she is rather quiet and thoughtful, but I can get on well with her. Lucy came down tonight for me to alter a polinase*, I hope it will fit her better now, it was put together badly. We had a fight before she went away, I soaped her face, she pulled my hair down and we had each other down on the floor.

Thursday July 19th

Lily came down for me tonight, we went up to the course to hear the band, we saw the Miss Palmers, what fun we had talking about Belvoir, I was ashamed of myself laughing so much on the course. They asked us where we was going on Bank Holiday, they would be jolly to go out with, but I must not make any arrangements yet. I can't find anything to say about today I am not half so happy as I ought to be, I wish somebody would say something or I am afraid my love will die out if we go on like this much longer. I wonder sometimes whether it would not be better for me to be an old maid.

Friday July 20th

I am ashamed of the money I am getting, we seem worse off for work than ever, what ever shall we do. I came to work early this dinnertime so I did not see George, I bet he comes in tonight although I do not know yet. He came about nine, how late he does come, I don't like it but I can't say anything. He had another lesson, I think he reads the notes well considering it's the first time he has tried. I will do all in my power to try and teach him. He wants to go by another half day trip, I can see through him but I shall not go about with him too much till things are settled.

Saturday July 21st

Polly Dilly told me today she did not know till this morning as I went to Skegness with a young man, I tell her she must be mistaken. I went out with Mother this afternoon, we met Father and he given me some money to buy a Macintosh, I was surprised and I have given Mother some money towards a jet Albert*, she wanted one bad enough. It is wet tonight so I have not gone for Lily to go out and I don't think I shall go now because it is eight o'clock. Father came home wet through about nine o'clock, I thought I was going up for eggs but I shall not go now, it pours with rain. I wish somebody was here but perhaps he has something else to do, bother it!

Sunday July 22nd

Father went to Skegness this morning, the house does seem miserable without him. I don't know what we should do if he was to go for good. Mother and I intended to go out in the morning but it poured with rain. We went to the Flower Service in the afternoon, we had a walk after, then had our solitary tea. I went to church at night, the Vicar of St. Mark's preached, I don't care much for him. I went to meet Lily, we saw George in Rutland Street, he did not see us. I will tell him about it, we had a walk on the course, it was nearly ten when I got home.

Monday July 23rd

I met George this dinnertime, he given me a note to give Elly for Arthur, I was rather surprised. He asked me if I should be at home at night as he thought of coming in, he came soon after eight, he said he was a good mind to come in on Saturday night, I was wishing he would come, but that did not bring him. Father saw him down Belgrave Gate on Sunday night, he (George) thought he might see some of us. He told me something about writing some letter, I cannot

Bradgate Park, Leicestershire, showing the ruins of Lady Jane Grey's house. *(Leicester City Council)*

understand it all, yet he did not say who he was writing to, I should like an explanation of the subject. The schoolchildren from Margaret's school went to Bradgate* today, I almost wish I had gone with them, but perhaps it is all for the best.

Tuesday July 24th

I am getting on dreadful bad at work again, I feel inclined to get a fresh place, they are docking the work down so. Lily came down, we went in the Market Place to hear the Band and we met George. He came and spoken to us, but he left us about eight to go to his club, Lily wondered if he was tired of his band, so I explained it to her. Mother tells me there is going to be some settlement, I wish to goodness I knew what it was, I should like to get out of this mist. We were disappointed in the Band it seemed to play so low as we could not hear it, we saw the Miss Palmers so we went on the Course. There has been some races, the town is so busy.

Wednesday July 25th

I met George this dinnertime, he said he should come in tonight, I thought perhaps he would come in, he came about eight, he went into Staples* before he came in our house, he did not tell me till the following Sunday. It did not seem to make him any cooler towards me, he was more the other way, he told me Alice was one and twenty she looks younger than that. I wonder sometimes if she has ever cared for him its hard to tell over such things. Who would have thought as I cared for him when I went to school, I should think it would surprise him if he was to know.

Thursday July 26th

Lily came down for me and we went to hear the Band, we saw the Miss Palmers again, we had some rare fun again. The youngest Miss Palmer is very good company but Lily says she is such a girl to make fun of people and she does not like that. When we got into Belgrave Gate we met George, I think that was done accidently on purpose, I may be wrong. The three of us came down Belgrave Gate, we left Lily and he came home with me, he told me as he should not come in the house, I said very well. We stood talking for a little while, he hoped I should enjoy myself on Saturday, I forgotten to say he raised his hat when we left Lily, I did like him for it.

Friday July 27th

This is the first night I have had to myself this week, it is about time I settled down to work, I have got plenty to do. I did some cleaning and got my things together ready for Saturday, I do hope it will be fine, if we don't go the children will be disappointed. George asked me if I thought Arthur would go to Leamington sometime, I can see what he is aiming at, I should be glad if they should get friends. I am always writing about George, if any one was to read this diary, they would think I had got George on the brain, so I have in a sense.

Saturday July 28th

Eliza and I have taken her class to Evington this afternoon, how pleased the children were, they romped and shouted to their hearts content. I was just in my glory because I love children, especially when I can play with them, everything was a success, I should like to go again. We were in Evington Lane when we met Arthur, we had hardly shaken hands with him when George was close to us, we did not know that either of them were coming so it was a big surprise. We got the children off, then the four of us had a walk round the Fosse*, that is the first time I have had with him, I mean in that way and I hope it will not be the last. He came home with me and had a practice, not for long though. I don't know whether I shall see him tomorrow.

Sunday July 29th

There has been such a bother this morning about the coffee, I hate rows it makes one feel so miserable. Mother did aggravate Father, it seems as though she does not go the right way to get round him, I should try to win my husband if I had got one. I went to school this afternoon, Mrs Clayton is going away for a month's holiday, Miss Dunmore will take the class, I don't like that. I went to church at night Mr Clayton preached a very good sermon on "Intemperance". I had a walk with Lily, I felt rather disappointed as I did not see George, but perhaps he will come when he has nothing else to do.

Monday July 30th

I have passed a miserable day with my work, my machine has gone wrong, it makes me feel inclined to leave and yet I should not like to leave all of my old friends. I am so stiff after our romp on Saturday, Eliza made me laugh this dinnertime, she was using her umbrella to get upstairs, then Lucy gave her a gentle lift behind. I must leave you now my diary as George has come, I will continue part of my Monday's doings, it is Thursday now. How I neglect you now, I am not nearly so constant as I was at first. George had another lesson, he seems to take to the music well considering what little time he has had at it, he says it is hard work, he must have Patience.

Tuesday July 31st

I am going to have the stitch of my Wilcocks and Gibbs machine made larger, that will be a great help to me. Mr. Jackson says it is to go by steam. I shall like that, it will not be such hard work. I went out with Eliza to buy a macintosh, I did not think of staying out for long but we changed our minds and had such a nice walk. We were talking pretty well too because Father passed us, and we did not see him, he said we were busy. We stood talking against Countess Street for a long time, Arthur and his cousin nearly passed us, they turned back and stopped a few minutes, it was about ten when I got home.

August

Wednesday August 1st

I met George this dinnertime, he said he should not be able to come in very early tonight as he had some work to finish. When I got home I helped Mother make some jam, I rather liked that, we are all getting friends at home now, how much better it seems to be friendly. It was a quarter to ten before George came, I really thought he was not coming at all. He said as he had promised he had better come late than not at all, he had been working down Willow Street till half past nine, he tells me now when he is coming in, perhaps its because he has not seen me at Monday dinnertime.

Thursday August 2nd

Elly asked me this morning if George had not pleased me last night as I seemed so half hearted. I did feel quiet, perhaps it is because of the work, I am tired of that place, I left off about four this afternoon, nothing to do, it's just as though we cannot get on for long together. I was just in the humour for music so I had a good long practice, then I tried to prepare the lesson for Eliza's class on Sunday, I feel afraid of taking it. Lily came for me tonight we went on the course, the band played some nice tunes. We saw the Miss Palmers just before the band had done playing, we had a bit of fun, we left them against Conduit Street, I do feel so tired tonight.

Friday August 3rd

I have not met George these last few dinnertimes, he came in earlier than I expected him, I was cleaning the pictures and had got the window to clean, I could not while he was here. He wanted to know if I was going out this Bank Holiday, I told him Lily wanted me to go to Cleethorpes and I didn't know whether I should, he would like to go. He would like to go everywhere I mention but he don't, he is not quite sure when he will come back from home. He asked me if I had been to Melton Mowbray, I thought he was very affectionate as usual before going to his own home.

Saturday August 4th

I stayed at home this afternoon, I quite thought he would call in to bid us goodbye, well he did not so it don't matter. I suppose he was going to the station to meet his sister about half past two, perhaps he would go on with her. Father has asked him to bring her here, I think they will think we are pushing ourselves in their way too much, I wish for some things they had let it alone for a bit. I went down to Lily's rather earlier than usual as she wanted to go shopping, we afterwards had a walk on the course. I have made my mind up to go to Cleethorpes on Monday, I mean to enjoy myself while I am young. Father has given me 3 shillings for my train fare.

Sunday August 5th

I went to Harvey Lane School to take Eliza's class and I feel disgusted with myself, I could not explain the lesson as I should have liked to have done, I will never undertake such a thing again. I had tea at Mrs Small's, Miss Houghton was there, I went to church with them afterwards. Mr Noels preached, he was their curate some years ago. We had a walk afterwards, I can't help thinking about that class.

Monday August 6th

I got up at about five o'clock this morning, Father got the breakfast, he is good when I am going out. I met Lily about six, Mother and Father went to the station with us, Father got our tickets. Lily and I could not get in the same carriage as the rest, we had a few showers at Cleethorpes, it was a dull day. Lily and I had a ride on the donkeys, they did give us a shaking, I did enjoy it, I laughed till I nearly fell off the donkey. After tea both of us went in a small boat on the sea. Oh dear, I was sick, I did feel so bad I wished I had not gone on. I enjoyed myself in a quiet sort of way, it was after one when we got in Leicester. Mother and Father came to meet me, I was glad to get home once more.

Tuesday August 7th

I went to work this morning about half past eight, I feel rather tired this morning. I think we shall have half a day's holiday, well I hope so, Elly has not come, Miss Ross tells me she was asleep when she asked me to come out of home and she told us not to come back after dinner. I had a walk with Mother and Father this afternoon. Mrs Dove called while we were having tea, we went down the Park with her after. I should think George is not coming back till tomorrow, perhaps he has something else to do instead of coming here. I am sick of this game, I wish I could give it up altogether.

Wednesday August 8th

We worked till seven o'clock tonight, Mother came to meet me out of work, I went with her to buy a new bonnet. George came in soon after eight, I asked him if he enjoyed himself, I think he said not very well. He was talking a great deal about Kate, I think he thinks a lot about her. I feel such a nasty disagreeable girl and I think he can see such a difference between the two of us. He did not say anything about having any music and I did not. I believe I was rather funny with him, well, he should say something then I should be alright.

Thursday August 9th

Lily came down for me, we went to hear the band, we met Eliza and Arthur, I feel disgusted with Lily, she thinks him a funny fellow and she shuddered when we met them. She thinks he has a gruff voice, I did not answer her, she would think I did not like it. I think he is a nice fellow, if it was her friend perhaps it would alter the case. I should not like Eliza to know, she would be vexed. I should not be surprised if there is not something wrong in George, I should liked to have seen him tonight, I like him ever so much better, I should think absence does not make my heart grow fonder.

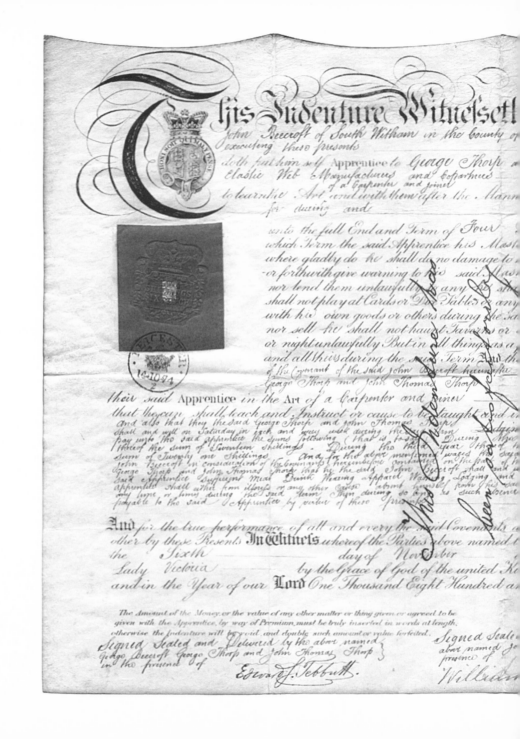

This Indenture Witnesseth

John Beecroft of South Witham in the county of ... executing these presents

doth put himself Apprentice to George Thorp ... Elastic Web Manufacturers and Copartners of a Carpenter and joiner

to learn the Art and with them after the Mann... for during and

unto the full End and Term of Four which Term the said Apprentice his Mast... where gladly do he shall do no damage to ... or forthwith give warning to his said Mast... nor lend them unlawfully any ... sh... shall not play at Cards or Dice Tables or any with his own goods or others during the sai... nor sell he shall not haunt Taverns or ... or night unlawfully But in all things as a ... and all this during the said Term And th... of the Covenant of the said John Beecroft hereinafte... George Thorp and John Thomas Thorp

their said Apprentice in the Art of a Carpenter and Joiner that thereon shall teach and Instruct or cause to be taught and in... and also that they the said George Thorp and John Thomas Thorp shall and will on Saturday in each and every week during the ... Term ... pay unto the said apprentice the same following (that is to say) During the ... thereof the sum of Seventeen Shillings. During the third year other of the sum of Twenty one Shillings. And for the abovementioned wages the sa... John Beecroft in consideration of the Covenants hereinbefore contained on the part of George Thorp and John Thomas Thorp that he the said John Beecroft shall and ... said apprentice sufficient Meat Drink Wearing Apparel Washing Lodging and ... apprentice shall absent form illness or any other cause absent himself from his sai... any time or times during the said Term then during so long as such absence ... payable to the said Apprentice by virtue of these present...

And for the true performance of all and every the said Covenants ... other by these Presents In Witness whereof the Parties above named t... the Sixth day of November Lady Victoria by the Grace of God of the united K... and in the Year of our Lord One Thousand Eight Hundred an...

The Amount of the Money, or the value of any other matter or thing given or agreed to be given with the Apprentice, by way of Premium, must be truly inserted in words at length, otherwise the Indenture will be void, and double such amount or value forfeited.

Signed Sealed and Delivered by the above named George Beecroft George Thorp and John Thomas Thorp in the presence of

Edward S. Tebbutt.

Signed Seale... above named jo... presence of

William...

That George Beecroft aged Seventeen years son of ... Lincoln with the consent of his said Father testified by his ... John Thomas Thorp both of Leicester in the County of Leicester ... an Apprentice to serve from the day of the date of these presents ... from thence next following to be fully complete and ended **During** ... faithfully shall serve their secrets keep their lawful commands every ... said Masters nor ... to be done of others but to his Power shall tell ... of the same he shall not waste the goods of his said Masters ... commit fornication nor contract Matrimony within the said Term he ... unlawful Games whereby his said Masters may have any loss ... Term without Licence of his said Masters he shall neither buy ... houses nor absent himself from his said Masters service day ... Apprentice he shall behave himself towards his said Masters ... George Thorp and John Thomas Thorp in consideration of such service and ... doth hereby Covenant with the said John Beecroft that they the said ... which they useth by the best means ... finding unto the said Apprentice sufficient Meat Drink ... all other Necessaries during the said Term ... the sum of Fifteen Shillings - During the second year ... of Nineteen Shillings - and During the fourth year thereof the said ... to wire Sixty ... per week - And the said ... George Thorp and John Thomas Thorp doth hereby Covenant with the said ... the continuance of the said Apprenticeship find and provide unto and for the ... necessaries - And it is expressly understood and agreed that if the said ... service or refuse or neglect to perform his work for his said Masters at ... or neglect shall continue no allowance whatsoever shall be paid or ... Agreement ... of the said Parties bindeth himself unto the ... Indentures interchangeably have put their Hands and Seals ... on the Thirty eighth Year of the Reign of our Sovereign ... of **Great Britain** and **Ireland** QUEEN Defender of the Faith ... seventy four.

George Beecroft
John Beecroft
George Thorp
Jno. T. Thorp

... Delivered by the ...
Beecroft in the ...

Lovell

George Beecroft's indenture.
He was apprenticed in 1874 to
George and John Thomas
Thorp of Friday Street in
Leicester.
The indenture is also signed by
George's father, John Beecroft.

81

Friday August 10th

Our washing machine* came this dinnertime, Father asked me to tell George to come in if I met him, I did not see him so therefore I could not tell him. He came at night to look at the washing machine, I should think he is going home again tomorrow. They are all going to meet as his sister is at home. Father told him Kate might sleep with me if she would like to come over, he thanked him. I wonder how we should get on together, perhaps she would not like me, I am such a nasty thing but I did feel more gracious tonight if I may term myself so.

Saturday August 11th

I went out with Mother about six to fetch her bonnet, I do like it and I think it suits her very much. I afterwards went down for Lily, H. Staples was there, we went on the course and we were talking what we should like to be married in if we were married at all. Lily would like a Cream Cashmere dress, wreath and fall*. Kate would like the same dress and a hat, I should like the same but I don't think the cream dress would suit me, I should rather like a Ruby Silk. Lily thinks a wreath and fall would suit me best as I look better without my hat.

Sunday August 12th

It was my turn out this morning but I did not go. Mrs Moore came in and hindered me from cleaning. I went school in the afternoon, Miss Dunmore taken the class, she had a lot to say on "Christ's temptation". I had a walk with Father down the park, I went to church at night and afterwards had a walk with Lily.

Monday August 13th

I met George at one o'clock, he stopped me, I was agreeably surprised. I asked him if his sister was coming over this week, he told me she was, but he would come in tonight. He came about half past eight and brought some walnuts for pickling, some cheese and gooseberries. He has either left his pocketbook at his sister's or lost it, he was showing them something (I should like to know what that something was), he does not remember any more about it. He has asked me to go up the course with him and his sister on

Thursday night, I am going to meet them. He said I might call at Mrs Grace's*, I told him I did not like that and I would much rather meet them, I do feel different to last week.

Tuesday August 14th

We had such a lark this breakfast time, I gave Mother a gentle push and she slipped off her chair on the floor, how we did laugh to see her sitting so comfortable on the floor. We are dreadfully short of work yet, I don't know what we shall do, I met George at seven, he has some work to do for Mr Tebbut, I think he does too much work. Mother and I had such a game over those walnuts we have got to pickle. While I am writing here she came in softly and frightened me ever so, then I bundled her out. She has tested the washing machine today, I am sure she has got her washing done quicker. I wish Father would come home as I think it is time for bed.

Wednesday August 15th

I mean to do some work tonight and get a bit tidy for Miss Beecroft coming. I had not got far with my work when George came walking in. I was surprised as he was going to be so busy, but the wood had not come for him to do Mr Tebbut's work, I tell him he works too many hours. We wanted to sing a few songs and he persuaded me to help him sing "Love at Home", I bet he will ask me to sing it tomorrow night. I do not like him for coming so unexpectedly, he quietly walked out of the front way as Father came in the back, he said Father would wonder how it was as he did not meet him (how sharp he is).

Thursday August 16th

I dare not think about him tonight, it gives me the belly ache. I was rather behind time and I met George and his sister in Causeway Lane. I could not tell anyone how I felt, I did not wait for a second introduction. We went on the course to hear the band, it was a beautiful night, we spoken to Eliza and Arthur. We came home and had supper, then we had some music, it was about two o'clock before we went to bed. George has made his sister a present of a bible, it is a beauty. He wanted me to call in Mrs Grace's with them but I would rather stay out, I do like his sister, she soon began to call me ADA, that pleased me. I should have liked her to of stayed longer, I think she would teach me to be a better girl, she did not want much persuading to sing, I want so much asking.

Friday August 17th

We went down the park before breakfast, we were up before seven so we did not have much of the bed. George came in for breakfast but he did not have it with us. We afterwards went shopping, we met A. Staples, the news would soon spread, we came down about eleven and Kate had some Luncheon. George asked me to go up to the station with them, I did not refuse, he asked me to go into Mrs Grace's again and I would not, I think it is best not to yet, I hope Kate will come again sometime. I got home about one o'clock, then I went to work in the afternoon. G. was here at night, he came in to thank mother for her kindness, he did not stay long and he went out the back way.

Saturday August 18th

We are all ready to go to Evington again, there is a party of seven, it was a beautiful day. Some little boys went part of the way with us, they helped us over the stiles and when we got to our favourite field, we had a game of rounders with them. We went in the church, a young lady was playing the organ, it is a nice little place. I had a misfortune and lost my bracelet, I am so sorry as it was a present from Mother, I am afraid I shall not hear anything about it again. Elly's young man came to meet her, I got home about nine, we left three of the girls behind, they all want to go again and we all enjoyed ourselves very much.

Sunday August 19th

I went down the park this morning, I had a book with me, it is such a beautiful day. I went to the class in the afternoon, we had Miss Dunmore for our teacher. I afterwards came home and got the tea ready, Mother and Father had gone down to the park. G. came to tea, we are getting used to him now, he asked me if I was going to St.

The Pavilion, Abbey Park. *(Leicester City Council)*

Margaret's Church and if I was going to meet Lily. I did meet Lily and Kate to my sorrow, I have never come across such ignorance in my life. They were talking secretly about Albert while I was there. I think Kate was the worst of the two for afterwards Lily tried to drag me into the conversation, but it will not pay Lily.

Monday August 20th

I do feel idle this day, I don't know what is the matter with me, I should like a holiday and go to Kirby*, ain't I a bad girl. None of the girls have got my bracelet, so there is no doubt but what I have lost it, I have not told Mother and Father yet, they will think I am careless. I think I had better leave off writing as I expect G. every minute and I don't want him to see me with my desk out every time or he will perhaps think something. He can't think as I write about him as much as I do, he came before nine, we had some fun. He knocked my hand and filled my mouth with chalk. I tell him I will pay him back, he was trying to play, I tell him he wants more practice. If I knew what his intentions were I should ask him to come and practice.

Tuesday August 21st

I have asked Eliza to come down tonight and I think Arthur will come too, I met George at night and told him they were coming. He said it was his club night, bother the club, it would have been so nice for him to have come as well. Of course, when they arrived Arthur and Mother began talking in their old style. I felt ashamed, Mother knows about my bracelet, Eliza was asking me about it, she looked astonished, I am glad she knows, I don't think I could have told her myself. We were laughing and joking at supper time, I nearly choked once or twice, Arthur wanted to fetch some more ale but we would not let him.

Wednesday August 22nd

I have promised M.A. Fowler I will go to school with her tonight, we have all got to settle about Mrs Clayton's present but when I got home at dinnertime Father said I might go with him to the Opera House, I told him I had promised to go out. Well, he said George was going, they are playing "The Silver King", I suppose it is a grand piece, I think I shall go now. One or two parts are so touching I shed a tear but I don't think they saw it, I hope not, it makes a person feel rather silly to weep when men are by. G. did not come in, he stopped against the church, I was rather disappointed but it was very late.

Thursday August 23rd

I am bothered dreadfully with my work today, I wish I was out of it sometimes. I met George this dinnertime and stopped him, I don't think he felt inclined to stop, I shalln't do it again in a hurry. I hardly think he would have stopped, perhaps he did not feel in the humour, I did feel vexed. He did not say much and then to finish with he said he must go. I won't stop tonight if I meet him at seven. I went on the course with Lily tonight, it was dusk before we got to the course, I got on capital with Lily alone. This time last week I was in somebody else's company, it is getting on for eleven o'clock and I wish I felt in a better temper, I am sick of this game.

Friday August 24th

My poor old diary, you have been neglected for more than a week. I am writing this on Sept. 3rd, but I must try and remember what has passed, my hand trembles, I can hardly write. Well, I went to work this morning, I was bothered with my work and did not feel well at all, I had got the Diarrhoea, I often have it lately. I stayed at work as long as I could then Elly advised me to go home till after dinner, so I came. They all had half a day's holiday, it was a good thing for me as I should have gone back, I was so sick and bad in the afternoon. George came in at night, he was reading to me and seemed so affectionate. Oh, how hot and feverish I am he remarked, then he went home earlier, then I went to bed.

Saturday August 25th

I felt a little better when I got up this morning, I was going to try to go to work this morning but I soon felt bad again so I had to give it up. In the afternoon Mother went to Mr Butler's*, he gave her some medicine. George called in at two o'clock, he is working this afternoon. The medicine did not relieve me, I was in such pain so Mother went again to Mr Butler's, he changed it. About seven Aunt Kilby brought George's sister to our house, Mrs Beecroft wanted to see George and did not know where to find him. She stayed to tea and George came in too, I could not speak to her I felt so ill, she would think me unsociable.

Sunday August 26th

Worse again this morning, Mother fetched Doctor Lancaster, he said it was a touch of the English Cholera*. Mrs Beck was very good to me, she made me some bran bags and stayed with me some time, Eliza and Arthur came to see me after tea and George, Lily brought me some Blanc Mange but I was to ill to eat it. Lily came in the afternoon as well, Mother is running about I am afraid she will be ill next.

Monday August 27th

I do not feel much better this morning, the Doctor came but he does not say much. Eliza and Lucy came this dinnertime, A. Baker sat with me in the afternoon, she had tea with Mother. I am not to have anything to eat till the complaint has left me. While they were here having their teas I was taken ill, it was the worst attack I had during my illness, I thought I should have died. I think the others were frightened, I could see Mrs Beck, Lily and Annie crying, they did seem in a way. G. came about seven, I was much better then. Lily was feeding me with arrowroot during the night, when she went home G. took her place, he was afraid of spilling it but he did not.

Tuesday August 28th

I had rather a bad night, George came at breakfast time and brought me such a beautiful bunch of flowers as ever I had seen, I do feel proud of them, I don't know how to thank him for them. Eliza and Lucy came at dinnertime, I am so much better. Father told her I was going to get up tomorrow, I think I have got the turn for the better now. George came in till after eight, he had promised to go out so he had to leave me early. I am not quite certain, but I think Lily and Annie stayed with me.

Wednesday August 29th

I remember George called in at breakfast time, the Doctor said this morning that I was out of danger, that is good news. He is going out of town, so he said he should have to get Dr Bell to call, it is his brother in law, I wonder what kind of a gentleman he is. I think I had Annie and Lily to see me, George stayed with me all night, I mean till about eleven o'clock.

Thursday August 30th

George came again this morning, I think it is a very good of him, I had no idea I had so many friends till I had this illness. I don't think I had many visitors this day, Lily came till she had to meet Kate, Oh I forgot, Kate came to see me one dinnertime and Patty Hurst and P. Dilley came one morning. George came till about half past eight, he had to go and practice. It was tonight as Eliza sent Arthur, she came herself last night till about nine, then she was going to meet him. I don't feel well tonight, I am glad they all went away early, if they get me out of bed it brings one of my bouts on so quickly. Grandfather Hyde stayed with us today, he came upstairs.

Friday August 31st

George came again at breakfast time, he waters my flowers, this is the second morning Dr Bell has been, I like him very much he talks to me so friendly. Father sent a note to Aunt Partridge this morning, so she came in the afternoon. Lily came after tea then Elly came, she has been least of all my friends, she did not stay long, then Annie came. Lily, Annie and George were all upstairs together, we had such a nice long chat, Lily did the principle part of the talking. G. thinks she has got a tongue, she generally finds plenty to talk about, she goes out such a lot. I thanked G. for my flowers, I forgot which day it was, but I think I showed my affection, perhaps it is all for the best.

September

Saturday September 1st

G. came at breakfast time, he says my flowers have faded, the Doctor says I must get up this afternoon, I am pleased. I got up about three and had a fire lit in Mother's room, nobody came to see me this afternoon. George came after six and directly he came Lily came, but she stayed down for a little while, then G. went away for an hour or two. Lily stayed with me, it was wet, she could not meet Kate. George came again soon after nine, I kissed him for the first time tonight, he blessed me after. Oh how I love him, I said my watch was fast like me, but he took it to himself for he asked me if I thought he was fast.

Sunday September 2nd

George came again this morning before church time, he kissed me and he put his face against mine for it to be returned, but I did not return it, so he said he thought I had forgotten. Mrs Moore came to see me and brought me a cake, George came to tea. Miss Bellward and Miss Tompson brought Mrs Clayton's present for me to look at it, it is a brass inkstand. After tea G. was telling me about the sermon they had in the morning, the text was "God is Love". Then he asked me if I could love him, Oh Dear, I did not know what to say, so I told him I thought so. He said there was a difference in our ages but that did not matter to anybody else if we were satisfied.

Monday September 3rd

I do feel happy today, the idea of having someone to care for me is not a trifle, how I love him. I should like to tell him but I shall not yet. I told him how young and inexperienced I was, he said if I liked we might wait a little longer as he would not be able to come on Saturday because of the club, but I should not mind about that. He came in this dinnertime, I have had a deal of happiness during my illness, I ought to be thankful, the Doctor came for the last time this morning I hope; I am to go and see him on Wednesday. P. Dilley had tea with us, Lily and Ellen came after tea, it is the first time Ellen has been here. George came soon after they had gone, then my cousin A. Partridge came, after that Eliza and Arthur came. G. asked me if I had thought about that as he had asked me, I hardly know how to answer him, he asked me about joining the church as a member.

Tuesday September 4th

I am going out today for the first time, how glorious. I called to see Mrs Cooper this morning, it is not far but I felt so tired when I got there, she was very pleased to see me. George called this dinnertime, he brought me some scented mint, I shall keep that. I went to see Mrs Baker this afternoon I surprised them as well as Mrs Cooper, they did not expect to see me out so soon, they seemed very pleased to see me and pressed me to stay to tea, I did enjoy it. Annie went out with me after tea and brought me home about seven, Eliza came down at night, she had not been here long before Elly came and gave me an invitation to tea tomorrow afternoon. I shall have plenty of places to visit, I feel so tired with going out, I am afraid I am doing too much.

Wednesday September 5th

I got up for my breakfast this morning, I can relish it so much better. I don't feel very well this morning, I am afraid the complaint may return and I don't want that. I am staying at home this morning then I shall feel more able to go out this afternoon. G. called this dinnertime, I was in the living room so we all talked together. Mother went with me to the Doctor's this afternoon, I don't think I shall go again as I am getting better. I afterwards went to Elly's for tea, I do feel sorry for her, she does seem miserable, I came home about seven. I met Miss Oram, they are saving some samples till I go back. Lily came down, she is here when George is here and she did not go away till about half past nine. He has asked me to go out with him tomorrow.

Thursday September 6th

I stayed in this morning then I shall be more fit to go out this afternoon. George came about two o'clock, he showed me a letter he had started to write to me and he had not the courage to finish it. We had a nice walk down the park and over some fields, I did enjoy it and felt so much better. He taken my arm for a little time, then it rained, he asked me to take his. When we were coming back we met Christ's Church Schools, C. Kilby was among them and E. Small, they both looked surprised. Eliza and Arthur came about nine, they were late but we all enjoyed ourselves, I think I am so happy, I hope it will last. George has given his consent for me to tell Mother about what he had asked me.

Friday September 7th

I told Mother about going out with him and she has no objection, she says she thinks Father would be quite willing. Father and George have gone to London today, I feel quite contented and do not mind at all. Elly came down directly after dinner, her young fellow has gone to the races, we went out about half past three, Mother went with us, Elly left us at the top of the New Walk* so Mother and I had a walk round the course, the last race was on when we got there. We got home about six and had our old maids tea, it does seem strange with Father out, but I enjoyed myself in a quiet sort of way. I gradually get better each day, I think I have got on well since I began to go out, I ought to be very thankful for it all.

Saturday September 8th

Father got home about three, we did not sit up for him but we heard him come home, he has enjoyed himself and so did George. He came in this dinnertime and asked me to go and hear the band tonight. I went into the Market with Eliza, her friend P. Smith's Father is very ill, I am so sorry. We went to hear the band, Mother and Father went with us, we saw Eliza and Arthur and a lot more of our girls, the news will spread about me and George, I don't care and he says he don't. We had a walk after, I am so happy, then we had our supper, he wanted to know if I had told my Mother, I told him I had. He is going to Staples for tea tomorrow, I do not mind at all, I feel as though I can trust him, that is worth something.

Sunday September 9th

I had a walk as far as the Cemetery with Father, then I left him to go to the garden as I could not get as far, I called to see Annie about going to Kirby on Tuesday. I met George in High Street he brought me home, I went to school in the afternoon, Mrs. Clayton has got back, she asked me if I was better. Elly met me out of school we had a walk down the park and saw A. Beck with two girls, if I was Elly I should give him up, she is too good for him I reckon. I went to church at night, Mr. Lewis preached. I met George afterwards and had a pleasant walk.

Monday September 10th

It is a dreadfully wet day today, I can't get out, it makes such a long day. It cleared up about tea time so Father came in to tell me to take the Rates, so I went. Then I called in to see Elly, she has got on better than I thought she would about A. and the two girls. When I got home Lily was here and I found out I had not brought the receipt for rates away with me, Father was cross, it put me about ever so. Lily went away before George came, he was very nice and he was sorry as I had made a mistake but he said I should have to make the best of it. I told him about C. Kilby saying as she thought that was my chap when she met us on Thursday, he did laugh.

Tuesday September 11th

I did not go out his morning I felt so down hearted about that receipt and it is so very dull, I wish it was about four o'clock then I could go and see about it. I went out about three, had a walk till about four, then I called at the Rate Collector's office. Mr Pegg has saved it for me, bless that man, my heart is as light as a feather now. I went home and had my tea, then I called to see Lily, I stayed till after eight, Lily wonders if I am engaged, I tell her no, but she says I am as good as, so I can't blind her. George came soon after nine, he was pasting some music together, he makes himself at home more than he used to, I am so glad. I am more free with him than I used to be, I am getting to know him better.

Highcross Street. The High Cross was the site of the Wednesday Market until 1884. *(Leicester City Council)*

Wednesday September 12th

I called to see Elly again, I tell her I am always there, she is rather happy considering her circumstances. Then I went in the Cross Market* buying apples and afterwards called in Mrs Baker's, we are going to Kirby tomorrow if it is nice weather. I went up to Mrs Dove's to tea this afternoon, Mrs Cholaston was there, Mrs Dove's Mother, I felt rather awkward. I cannot think how it is, I should think I am a funny girl, I am always fancying people do not like me. I came away after six and I brought such a nice bunch of flowers with me. M.A. Fowler came about eight, I introduced her to Father we went to the meeting at the school to make arrangements for Saturday, I felt very quiet when I was there.

Thursday September 13th

I called for Annie and I met Mr Herrick in Church Gate, he asked me if I was better, I was rather disappointed, I thought I should meet George and I did not. We met H. Staples on the London Road and Mr Webster, he bid me "Good Morning", we got to Mrs Mason's about ten and I am so sorry, we found her in so much trouble about her husband, he drinks so sometimes and then comes home and ill uses her. It was a beautiful day, I think both of us enjoyed ourselves very much, we were out in the air nearly all the time. George came to meet us but he was rather late because he had to work till after seven. We had a nice walk after we met Annie and got home about nine. He came back after eleven to tell us Gascoine's factory* was on fire, so I went with him to see it, they were putting it out when we got there.

Friday September 14th

I shall be glad when I can go to work again it seems so dull at home, I went and bought some meat this morning and they said it was very nice. It is a most beautiful day, I must get out, I went of an errand for Father soon after dinner. When I got back I went in the Factory and Father weighed me, I have not lost much or I have got it up this last week, I weigh seven stone ten pounds. I went down the park afterwards and taken a book with me to read, it was delightful, I came home and had a very good tea, then about half past seven I had a walk with Father for about an hour.

Saturday September 15th

I had a walk round the Market this morning then I met Mother at Mrs Baker's, we came home loaded. George came in at one o'clock, he stayed till after two. He asked me for his Hymn Book, so he came in the parlour to sing a tune he wanted to learn. I called to see Eliza and she has surprised me, she told me that her and Arthur had parted, she has not seen anything of him since Wednesday. I tell her he will come tonight as it is only a lover's quarrel, I stayed too long and I was not ready when M.A. Fowler came for me. We had tea at the Coffee House* and all the presentations were made, Mrs. Clayton was very much surprised as she should have got one, it all ended well. There were a few young fellows after tea, I enjoyed myself very much and I had a pleasant surprise when I got home. G. was here having supper, I did like him for coming down like that, it makes me think he thinks about me.

Sunday September 16th

I have done something by going to the tea, I have sprained my ankle and I cannot walk, it is so painful this morning. I hope it will soon be better so as I can get out this afternoon. It takes Father all his time not to laugh at me. I went to school this afternoon, Mrs Clayton thanked us again for her present. I went down the park, afterwards I met Mother and Father, soon after George came up to us, he had tea with us. I went to Margaret's Church, G. went to his own, then I met him. He says Mr Taylor wants an introduction. Oh dear, and he tells me they are beginning to talk.

Monday September 17th

I started work this morning, it seems so strange, my little machine goes by steam now, I *like it much better, it is taking most of my time to talk, so I am not doing much work. I met G. at dinnertime he asked me how my ankle was, it was painful yesterday but it is much better today, I felt so tired that I left work at five. Eliza and Arthur have not made things square yet, he is longer about it than I thought he would be, she did not go to Chapel on Sunday. George came down rather earlier tonight, he asked me if I would like to go for a walk, that is what I have been longing for, so we went along the Groby Road, it was rather a pleasant walk to me. We met E. Bond and her young fellow, afterwards he saw Mother and she saw us, he had got my arm. Father was talking about the jerry* at the supper table, I did feel vexed at him, he did it all the more then.*

Tuesday September 18th

It does tire me coming to work, I am leaving off at five, G. has gone to the club tonight. Lily came down, we have decided to go to Scraptoft Church* on Sunday night. Elly came down about nine, she had been down to Eliza's and Arthur was there. I was pleased to hear that Elly soon shot off, then she called at our house, she said Miss Ross was going to her other sister's to sleep so I asked Elly to come back here. Lily and Elly had quite a discussion on religion, both of them got quite hot, they cannot get on at all. Elly went to London yesterday but she could not remember the names of the places she had been to. It was after twelve when we went to sleep, that shows what a lot we had to talk about.

Wednesday September 19th

George caught us up when we were going to work this morning, he raised his hat when he left us. I had to fetch those deeds back for Father as I took on Saturday, P. Dilley went with me. She does look bad, she is to go in the country if she wants to get better, they are so poor I don't know how they will afford it. George and I had a walk round Belgrave, I had got my silk jacket on, he said it was absurd of me as I might catch cold. He seems to have a deal of feeling for anyone, I do like him for it. I had a laughing fit on me, it is awkward as I cannot keep a straight face.

Thursday September 20th

I have had my feelings hurt this morning by Mr Webster, he said I had spoilt some smoking caps. I know the machine does not work as it ought, but it often does that and he has seen the caps. Perhaps he was in a bad humour, Mrs Short tells me not to take any notice of him, he does not care what he says when he is put out. He told Miss Ross not to give me the full price, the mean old wretch, I feel as if I could get another place, I have done bad this year. I met George at dinnertime, he said I looked tired, he don't know what trouble I am in, I stayed till seven tonight. I do feel tired when I got home. I left my umbrella on the machine, and Father told me to put it away, I did not the minute he told me so he started on me then and called me a stupid donkey, nice names from a Father. I had another good cry, I have cried a few times today, I am wretched.

Friday September 21st

There was a terrible thunderstorm after I had finished writing last night. Who should come down after practice but George, he though we should be frightened at the thunder and lightning. I think it was very thoughtful of him and I like him ever so much better for coming. He wants me to go to church with him tonight as it is St. Matthew's Day. I think I shall encourage him to go to church as it is a good thing, well, I went, and rather liked the sermon, it was more for the teachers. It is the first time I have been to church with him, I think it is much better for both to go to one place of worship as it seems to bring you together. He seemed very loving when we got home.

Saturday September 22nd

Miss Ross stopped me a halfpenny for those caps, but she has made it up double in another way so I have had the best of him. I was busy this afternoon, I did not get myself cleaned until after seven. George has gone to Enderby* with the Young Men's Association, Dr Buck explained to them about the quarries and granite stone, he enjoyed himself very much, he got down about eight. I did not bother about going out as he was rather tired, he wanted to know if I had been out, he thought I ought to have gone out in the afternoon. He was half asleep, I should think it was the fresh air. I made a small cake to give to P. Dilley and I have not had time to go in yet, I suppose *she is very ill indeed, I feel so sorry.*

Sunday September 23rd

I stayed at home this morning, Mother had a walk down the park. I went to school this afternoon, it is Harriet Thompson's last Sunday, she brought a text book for us to write our names in, Lily came to meet me out of school, she came down to tea and George came too. We started soon after five to walk to Scraptoft, we got to the church just before they started the service, Mr Rowlstone did not preach as he is away at Nottingham, I think it was the curate of St. Saviour's. We had a pleasant walk, it reminds me of Evington.

Monday September 24th

I feel happier at work today, I think it is about time. I just called in to see P. Dilley yesterday afternoon, she looked very ill indeed but they said she was very much better. I called again tonight but could not stay for long, I thought she looked better. George came about eight, we had a walk down Abbey Lane, he told me as A. Bond was going to be married. I am rather surprised, I thought it would have been Emma first. He told me another bit that surprised me in more than one way, Mrs Jordan had got twins. I knew nothing about it and he was talking to me as though he thought I knew. I felt rather silly, it was a good thing it was dark, I blushed so. I
helped him sing when we got home,
Oh yes.

Tuesday September 25th

Mrs Buck is going to send P. Dilley to Birstall Lodge* today, I am very glad as I think it will do her a world of good. E. Cooper and I went in at night to bid her goodbye, she seems lifted up to think as she is going away. Eliza came down to do some machining, Arthur came in for her, George called in as well, he had been working for Mr Hunt. He seemed so quiet while Eliza and Arthur was here, I wonder how it is. I should like to tell him about it, but I do not know how he would take it as yet, I do not know him sufficient for that. We had a sensible talk last night on religion, he shown me the form they have to go through for people that have not been christened when they were young.

Wednesday September 26th

Annie said perhaps she should come down tonight, I wish she would, but there is no dependence on her. I met G. this dinnertime, I thought he was rather light hearted, it might have been my fancy, he is going to bring me his Hymn Book for tomorrow night. Lily and I are going to St. Matthew's Harvest Festival if all is well. Elly wanted me to go there tonight, but I felt as though I did not want to go, so I would not promise her. It is just as I expected, Annie did not come. Father came home before ten o'clock, he has got a severe cold and the toothache very bad. I hope it will not last long on him as men seem rather impatient when they are ill.

Thursday September 27th

Father had to come home from work this morning, he has to be very bad to do that. I met George at two o'clock, he has lent me his Prayer Book and Hymns. I called for Lily at night and we went to St. Matthew's Church, we had to sit at the back, so to hear we had to listen attentively to the Rev. Canon Smith. I was interested in the sermon, Lily and George though it was too long, I own it was a long sermon, he was speaking of the final Harvest when we should all be gathered in. The church was tastefully decorated, some of the choir had a flower, George given me his. He tells me I want a deal of persuading to do something, I tell him I don't think so. Father is not any better, he has been in bed most of the day, his face is swelling more.

Friday September 28th

Father came home again this morning, he does not seem any better, it makes him irritable, I expect his face is so painful. I met George, he asked me how Father was, he has been in a great deal to see him, thoughtful George again. I wish I could be more like him, I think I had better try. He came in tonight to put a lock on the back door. He is rather playful before Mother and Father, sometimes it makes me feel rather silly. It was after eleven before he went away, he keeps late hours. Oh how I love him. I think sometimes it is wrong of me to love so much as something might happen to take him from me. I should like to know if he cares for me any more.

Saturday September 29th

I had a row with Mother when I got home this dinnertime, it was over some fish. We were both of us stupid, neither of us would put it in the oven. I thought after I ought to have gave in as it was Mother, I must be very disagreeable sometimes. It is such a wet day I don't think there will be any going out, Lily was to have come down this afternoon but it rained, so I went out with Mother. We called at Mrs Baker's, George did not come till about nine o'clock, I thought something had happened. We did not go out, Father was at home so we had a small family gathering.

Sunday September 30th

I went to St. Margaret's Church this morning, it is the Harvest Festival, it is something unusual for me to do. There was a Children's Flower Festival service in the afternoon, I called for M.A. Fowler and we both went. A. Beck was there morning and afternoon. George came to tea, A. Baker came after to go to church with me, Rev. Canon Mitchinson preached, I liked him very much. The church was very full, I was glad to see that, the singing went well. George met me after the service and we had a walk, when we got home Father was here, I like him to be at home, it seems so much nicer, it was half past ten when George went away.

October

Monday October 1st

I feel so very happy this morning, I have not any trouble of any sort just now. Father is much better, he went to work before breakfast this morning. I expect George every minute so I think I had better leave you now and see what occurs further on this evening.

Well, George has asked me to go home with him on Saturday, I asked him to excuse me this time, he says he does not want me to go against my will, I thought he was rather vexed over it, but it may only be my fancy. We had a walk but did not go far, he seemed as if he did not care to go out at all, Mother was not at home when he came. He mentioned to me about his sister Kate writing to me, he asked her to as he thought he should not have to write so often, I shall be glad to hear from her.

Tuesday October 2nd

I thought the singing went well at our church on Sunday night, but George told me last night that four of the trebles had been suspended for a few weeks through singing wrong. Two or three as I have asked seemed to think it went well so I am not the only one. George is going to the club tonight so I shall not see him, in fact he has not said when he is coming again. I did the ironing tonight and cut an apron out for Mother, I have begged one for myself from her. I think she brought it on purpose for me, I did sugar her up this dinnertime.

Wednesday October 3rd

I do go to work so late in the mornings, it is just as though I cannot break myself in to get early, it must be through Father going to work before breakfast. I suppose George has asked him to go home with him. I don't know whether Father will go, I wish he would, it might do him good. I met George at dinnertime, he said he should come in tonight, I almost thought he would. I was machining when he came, he said I was busy so he would sew a button on his coat, I could have laughed but I hardly dare. I thought he was in a bad temper, he seemed very independent, I was rather disappointed as we did not go out for a walk and I was longing to go.

Thursday October 4th

I started to go earlier to work then I stopped to talk to B. Cooke, she was telling me about the singing at church last Sunday night, so I was late again of course. George came down earlier tonight, we had a nice walk down the Occupation Road* and along Welford Road. He told me Father is going home with him on Saturday, I am so glad, it may do him good, and another thing, it will be an opening for me. Father wanted to know if I was going, George told him as he had asked me but I would not go, they thought I was shy and so I am, I hardly thought Father would go. George asked me if I should go up to the station if he could not get in tomorrow night, I said I should see, I feel happier today.

Friday October 5th

I was early this morning for the first time since I was ill, I think it is about time. I am getting on well with my money again this week, but I am afraid we are rather short of work. I went to Jacobs and Kennard's* this dinnertime with Elly to buy her sister a present. I did a bit of cleaning tonight, I did not think George would come but he popped in just before ten, rather late; Mother went upstairs so we had a bit of fun, he generally gets the better of me as he is the stronger. They are going to start about four tomorrow, Father says he has to go as I will not, he said that when George had gone. G. says I am to be good.

Saturday October 6th

I did some of the cooking this afternoon as Mother and I want to go out tomorrow morning. Then we both went shopping, we called at Mrs Baker's, I asked Annie to come down to tea tomorrow afternoon, but I think it is possible she will not come. I called at Mrs Biggs about seven, they were just going to have supper, I stayed and had supper with them, then Elly came home with me. Her young fellow is taking tickets at the Floral Hall*, she would have liked to have gone I think, but I did not care to go. We had a walk up the London Road. I feel so quiet and nasty tempered, I cannot think how it is, I must be a very disagreeable girl, I am nasty with Mother, then I am sorry for it. Elly slept with me.

Sunday October 7th

Mother and I had a walk on the cemetery this morning, it was about quarter past one when we got home, then we had to see to the dinner. So, I got that down me and I had to march to school soon after. I went to meet Annie but she was not there, so I jumped to the conclusion she could not come. Elly and Mr Beck came to tea, I feel so dull and quiet again, I wonder how it is. I left them and went to Church, I don't think Elly would go to church. When we got home from church George and Father was here, I was very glad to see them back again. We all had supper, then some music.

Monday October 8th

Father says how comfortable Mrs Beecroft made him and I think he enjoyed himself. G.'s sister lives in a nice house, her husband is a baker, I feel as if I want to know them now. I met George this dinnertime, he told me he should come in tonight, I did some machining when I got home tonight, I have got such a lot of work to do, I must do it before he comes at night. Mother went to the Temperance Hall, it is the Centenary of the Great Meeting Schools*, the scholars had a tea then there was singing afterwards. George came about eight, we began larking so it was about half past nine when we went out. He asked me if he should come in tomorrow night if he got his work done early, but he wonders if he is coming in too much. I tell him I do not think so. (I do not think I shall get tired of seeing him).

Tuesday October 9th

E. Cooper told me this morning they had another row last night over nothing, the motto is "True Love Never Runs Smooth", I should think that is the case with them. There was such a row when I got home this dinnertime, I rather think they are both in the wrong. Mother got quite out of temper and pulled Father's hair, he soon turned round on her then. I don't think Mother has the right way of managing him, I should try to make my husband love me. I was machining tonight, George came about nine, I did not think he would come. He told me he went as far as Staples but they were closed, so he did not go in. He went home earlier tonight, he thinks he ought to go before they turn out of the Public Houses.

Wednesday October 10th

We are not right at home yet, Mother seems to do everything to aggravate Father, I am sure she will not get on at all if she goes on like that, it makes me feel miserable. It was late before George came tonight, he told me after that he had been in to Staples. Eliza does not seem much better, I feel very sorry for her. He said I was rather dull, he wanted to know if I was not well, two or three times he asked me. I think it is through Mother and Father being as they are, so he begged me to tell him what it was. I did not want to tell him, but he got it out of me at last, he said I was not to trouble about that and make myself ill.

Thursday October 11th

K. Staples had a letter from Lily, she is coming from Nottingham tonight after eight. Kate asked me to go with her to the station to meet Lily, I don't know what I shall do yet. E. Cooper wants me to go to their house, I met George at dinnertime, he asked me if I was going down the fair* as he should about half past nine. He asked me last night as well, so I decided to go with Kate then go down the fair but it rained so hard I had to stay at home, well I did not care as I had plenty of work to do.

Friday October 12th

I saw P. Dilley this dinnertime, I don't think she looks so well again, I hope she will not go back again. She says she shall come to work on Monday, I think she will be very silly if she does. I met G., he says he shall have to come down tonight after he has done his work. He came through the fair about half past nine, I did not go I told him. He said there were a lot down there considering what a wet night it was. He came down after nine, we had such a lark, he was trying to get a needle case out of my hands and I would not give it up till I was obliged to, he said I was strong. He does not know whether his brother is coming yet. G. will bring him down in the afternoon if he comes.

Saturday October 13th

I was rather late going to work this morning so I met B. Cooke and we stood talking till half past eight, G. caught me up and said I should be rather late. When I got home Father told me G. had got a letter from his brother and he is coming down about four, well he came and G. introduced me, I did feel shy and know I blushed. Mr Beecroft seems very quiet, we went down the park, Mrs Baker's children were down, G. spoke to them. He asked me to go to Mrs Grace's with them to tea but I refused. When I got home Lily was here so I went out with her, I think she has found out she cares a little bit for Mr Caseley although she will hardly own to it. I know she has not told anyone too much about it as she has told to me. I left Lily and Kate in the fair soon after eight, G. and his brother came down to supper about nine. His train went away about eleven, I went up to the station with them, Eliza and Arthur were here when we got home, Arthur kissed Eliza when he was leaving her, I did feel so silly. I shook hands with G. while Mother was in the room.

St. Margaret's Church, interior.
(Leicester City Council)

Sunday October 14th

Eliza and I did not get to sleep till after two, we were talking of many things. Mother has got a very bad headache this morning so I got the dinner. I was late for school in the afternoon, but I went for all that. Mr Spencer went down the park with Father then they came to our house for tea, I introduced G. to him, they got quite friends, G. likes him. I went to Margaret's Church and G. went to his own, I feel much better if we both go together. I wish he would offer to go with me sometime without me asking him. I met him at night but it was so wet we came home, I was rather quiet with him, then I was sorry for it afterwards.

Monday October 15th

Eliza told me this morning how well she and Arthur got on yesterday, they never had such an understanding before. She will be able to tell me in a few weeks when they are going to be married. Arthur wishes her to make a confidante of me, so she says now she will expect me to help her in many things. Through Eliza talking it made me feel as though I would try to be happier tonight. George came in about eight, we could not go out because it was such a bad night, I think I did talk more. We had some fun, but I generally get the worst of it as he is the strongest. He asked me if I should like to go to the Opera House on Wednesday night, I said I should see, he would like to go, I suppose the music is so good.

Tuesday October 16th

I went up to Mrs Baker's this morning before I went to work to bid Mr Spencer "Goodbye", but he was not up. They sat up till two o'clock in the morning so they were all too tired to rise early. I am sorry I could not see him, I went down to Lily's tonight and we had a walk down the fair, it seems to get worse every year, there were not many people there and some of the shows had gone away. Lily is happier and lighter hearted tonight, she says she feels quite jolly, she wants me to go to St. Martin's School* on Tuesday night, there is a class for young women. I tell her I will go with her to see what it is like.

Wednesday October 17th

George has not sent word by Father about going to the Opera House as he said he might, I shalln't go unless I hear something. I met him at dinnertime and he asked me about it, I am going to meet him about seven. I liked it very much indeed but we could not understand because they sang in Italian. Miss Gaylord taken the part of Mignon well, George asked me if I wished I could sing as well as she did and whether I should make use of my voice then, I rather think I should. He told me as Mr A. Beck went away from the club early, G. told him he had better not go or he might catch it. I was so vexed at him deceiving Elly as he does that, I called him a deceitful beggar.

Thursday October 18th

I feel so happy today and did last night as well, they say if you try to make others happy you make yourself happy too, I do think that is the case with me. I tried to be as nice as I could last night and I am sure G. seemed happy, I have got a bit of a cold, he says I must take care of it, I met him this dinnertime, he asked how I was. I went to E. Cooper's at night, we were working, it is a long time since I was there last, Eliza shown me her new hat and jacket, I like them both very much. Mrs Cooper says I must take my young man there and she will tell me what she thinks of him. Eliza says it would be nice for him to come for me some Thursday night, I think he would have liked to see me tonight but I told him I was going out.

Friday October 19th

I met George this dinnertime, it was raining so I had to put my mackintosh on, I felt so silly when I saw him coming, he stopped and spoken, he said he should come in tonight. Eliza had some bad news to tell me, Arthur and his sister have had a row and he says he shall leave home but Eliza has persuaded him to stay instead of getting lodgings for a short time. She has told me that they thought of getting married somewhere about May, I think it may be sooner than that time. George came about nine and he was teasing me while I was reading, I shall begin with the same game. He has been what is commonly known as pumping me about Eliza and Arthur's wedding, he wants to know when it is coming off, he thinks I am helping to prepare.

Saturday October 20th

I went to work so light hearted this morning, Mother and Father are all right now, I think that makes me happier. Elly and I went shopping, I left her and called up at Mrs Baker's, Mrs Mason was there, she asked Annie and I to go next Thursday but Annie cannot promise. I afterwards called to see Mrs Dove, she seems in great trouble, her husband is coming home again for good, that makes three situations in three months. Then I went to Mrs Twigger's, her baby is a nice little thing, I could soon make friends with him. George came to meet me, I was rather late, we went up the London Road and we met Lily and Kate. George has bought a silk handkerchief for his sister Kate, it is her birthday next Tuesday, he got me to go in for it.

Sunday October 21st

Lucy Cooper went to church with me this morning, Mr Odell preached, we had a bit of a walk after and I met Father. I went to school in the afternoon, then I met Elly, we had a walk on the race course. A. Beck caught us up in Bond Street, I went to St. Margaret's Church at night then I met G., he did not say he was coming but I thought he would. We had a walk, he was rather quiet all the night, but when we got home he frightened me, he asked me for a glass of water, I thought he was going to faint he looked so bad, and there was nobody at home, I did feel so sorry for him.

Monday October 22nd

I went up town before one o'clock to buy a birthday card for G.'s sister, I asked him to send it with his present, he said he had no doubt she would be pleased to receive it. I was glad enough to send it but I wondered if he would think I was too forward. I met T. Bevins, he asked me if I should go over to Belgrave next Sunday, I said I should see. Mother has gone to a concert at St. Margaret's, it was getting on for nine o'clock when G. came, I began to wonder if he was coming at all. We did not go out, he did last night what he has never done before, he kissed me directly he came in, I thought he was very affectionate. I thought I was too heavy for him to lift but he carried me across the house, I wondered where I was going to.

OCTOBER   22 MONDAY [295–70]   10th Month 1883

(11ʰ 19ᵐ P.M.

I went up town before one o'clock to buy a birthday card for G. Sister I asked him to send it with his present She said no doubt she would be pleased to receive it I was glad enough to send it, but I wondered if he would think I was to forward I met T Bevins, he asked me if I should go over to Belgrave next Sunday I said I should see. Mother has gone to a concert at St Margrates It was getting on for nine o'clock when I came I began to wonder if he was coming at all. We did not go out, he did last night what he has not done before he kissed me directly he came in I thought he was very affectionate I thought I was to heavy for him to lift, but he carried me across the house I wondered where I was going to

23 TUESDAY [296–69]

Tuesday October 23rd

I met B. Cooke this dinnertime, she asked me if I was going to the Sewing Class at St. Margaret's, I told her I had promised to go out. I met G. as well, I asked him how his cold was, he does not seem well at all and he has hurt his finger. Lily came down for me and we went to the class for girls at St. Martin's School, we went in the Dictation Class, it was so simple we asked if we could go in the Grammar class next week, I did not like it at all. Lily has not had a letter from London yet, she has given it up till just before Christmas, I do think it so a mystery. She was quite lively last night, we did keep laughing when we were in the schoolroom.

Wednesday October 24th

Mrs Twigger did not come this afternoon as she promised so I expect it was the weather that kept her away, it was raining most of the day. George came earlier tonight, he said he should have come sooner and we could have a walk. Because we had arranged to go out it rained, so we stayed in and had some music, it is some time since we did have any. He persuaded me to sing with him without playing the piano, I can why he did that, I think he means to get me to sing when I go over to his home, but I do not think he will succeed. He would have liked me to have gone for a walk with him when he came out of practice, but I told him Eliza was coming, he said he would not come down and interrupt us.

Thursday October 25th

I asked Eliza to come down tonight, she wants to do some machining, when she was coming down she met George, she had such a great bundle with her, I suppose George is working till eight. I feel so happy somehow tonight, we had quite a pleasant conversation on many things. I thought perhaps George would call in but I suppose he went to church, he told me next time he came in that he peeped through the letter box. I was practicing some songs P. Poyner had lent to me. There was "The Gipsy Countess", "A Sweet Face At The Window" and "Rock Me To Sleep Mother". It was nearly eleven before Eliza went away.

Friday October 26th

I have earned more money this week than I have earned before in my life, it has made me feel quite good tempered. I met George this dinnertime, he told me he has got to work till eight tonight. He came in sooner than I expected him, of course he got a paper as soon as he arrived, that does aggravate me. As soon as he had done reading I had to put my work down, he said it was time I had done as it had gone ten. He tried to examine my work so we had a struggle over that, he did not get the work after all.

Saturday October 27th

I felt so giddy this morning when I got up, I thought I should have fainted, I did not feel well all morning. Eliza and I went on the cemetery this afternoon, I did enjoy my walk. When I left her, Father and I went off to buy some boots, I suppose George has had to go to Belgrave this afternoon, I should not be surprised if he did not go to the Lecture, but I had not been there many minutes before he walked in. I felt rather vexed as there were only about half a dozen women there, the lecture was by Mr Weatherhead on "Masks and their Wearers". We had a walk after, I was so disagreeable all the night with George, I shall go on too far some of these times. I must try and be different tomorrow, I am ever so sorry now, I told him I did not want him to come here against his will.

Sunday October 28th

Mother went out this morning, I went to the class this afternoon, then we went to the children's service. There were not many teachers there, I expect it is because the Oddfellows* went to a service to St. Martin's Church, George went as well. He came down to tea, he was so nice and I am sure I tried to be better, he asked me again to go to his church so I made up my mind to go, he went in the choir, I felt rather lonely. The sermon was by Canon Hole and a very good sermon it was too, we had a walk along the Melton Road and we had such a nice talk, I am so happy just now, I thought of our Belgrave walk.

Monday October 29th

I met B. Cooke this dinnertime, she was talking to me about A. Bond's wedding, they were married quietly on Saturday morning, all the girls thought it would be on Sunday, fancy, there is another of my school fellows gone. L. Cooper had to go home this morning, a block fell on her head and raised such a lump poor girl, it quite unnerved her. I suppose Lily had to go out of church last night she was ill, I think it was a bilious attack. George came late again tonight, he had been working, he asked me to stitch the sleeve of his shirt, I could not do it so well as I should like to. He was asking me when he was to come again and he said something I liked, it made me think he must care a little bit for me, he hoped he should see me again soon if he was not to.

Tuesday October 30th

P. Dilley has come back to work this morning, she looks better for her holiday, this time I hope she will keep well. I suppose George has gone to work at Belgrave today, I shall not meet him this dinnertime. Lily came down for me to go to school, we went into the advanced Grammar Class, both of us like it much better than dictation. We think of staying there, we had parsing and composition to do, I think they will be useful to me. Lily is much better she often enquires about Mr Beecroft, she has not had a letter from London yet, she is very fond of talking about Mr Caseley to me. She tells me all about the London flirtation, I think she likes him.

Wednesday October 31st

I finished Father's shirt, I bet there will be something the matter with it when he tries it on, well I have done my best, I can do no more. George came about half past eight, he turned the mangle for Mother, we had a walk, I thought George was very quiet, I wonder if he is getting tired of my company. I should like to ask him, perhaps I shall, or he might not be well. He asked me if I was going to Eliza's tomorrow night, I said "no", so he asked me to meet him about half past nine if it is a nice fine night. I said I would if he wanted me, he told me he should not ask me if he did not care for me to go.

November

Ada and George

Thursday November 1st

It is quite a November day, so dull and dreary it makes me feel dull. Eliza looks the same, I don't think she is very happy just now, she says she feels vexed, I expect it is over some little trifle. It is voting day and there was such a bustle this dinnertime. I saw the old "sand man" going to vote for the Tories. The two Liberal Candidates have got in for N. St. Margaret's Ward*. I thought I should like to meet George tonight so I went about half past nine. I thought he was more chatty and that made me happy so of course we could talk more. We had a walk, I should like to know how it was that he was so quiet last night. I had a good opportunity to ask him but I did not take the chance.

Friday November 2nd

I was with Eliza till eight o'clock tonight, we were talking about R. Butler, she sits against Eliza, she is a mean girl, I think Miss Ross will tell her what she thinks of her tomorrow. She has been selling some old buttons to one of the little girls for sixpence and I suppose they look as though they have been worn. George came in tonight but it was late, then he wanted the Free Press* directly he got in, I asked him if that was what he came for, he said "not exactly". I told him I should like to go to that lecture tomorrow night, he will meet me out.

Saturday November 3rd

Miss Ross talked to R. Butler, Becky began to smash the things about for a bit then she began to cry, she seems quite mute, none of the girls think much of her for her dirty tricks. I went out with Mother this afternoon and she lost me once, she was vexed when she found me again, George was working this afternoon. I went to the Museum Buildings, Mr Roberts lectured on "The Application of Art to Home Life". I thought it was very good advice for those people as wished to decorate a house. It was after nine when we came out, I told George it might be half past eight, so he had been waiting for me. He expected his brother so we went to meet the train, he had come by that train, I thought he might not come till tomorrow morning. They came down to supper, then we had some music, it was half past twelve when they went away.

Sunday November 4th

I promised Lily I would go to church with her this morning, but I did not get up, we got up so very late, then I had to help Mother. Annie met me out of school, G. and his brother-in-law came down to tea, I like him very much, we had some music, Annie and I went to church. George, Father and Mr Beecroft had a walk, they were at Mrs Baker's when Annie and I called after church, I was surprised to see him there, he thought I was. We all came down to supper, then about eleven George and I went home with Annie, I feel so happy, I only hope it will last, but I am afraid. I thought G. was very nice and looked nice today.

Monday November 5th

I had a letter from Kate this morning, she has told me in the letter when it is George's birthday, if I do not send him something now I think I shall look mean, I must see what Eliza says. I have decided on sending him a card, Eliza went with me to buy it, I written the address at Emery's and posted it there. I shown George the letter Kate had sent me, he had one too and some views of Penzance, she thought his birthday was today and it is not till tomorrow. We could not go out as it rained so, I thought he was very quiet again tonight, some of these times I shall ask him what is the matter with him, I do not like it at all, it soon freezes me. Mother went to Mrs Moore's for a short while, her little girl has caught the fever now, the boy is better now, I am so sorry for her.

Tuesday November 6th

I met George at one o'clock, he laughed, I should think he received the card this breakfast time if it went to the right house, I was not certain of the house. I was so anxious to get home, I thought Father would say something about it, but he did not. He said G. had a letter from his Mother, perhaps he would not tell me because I did not tell them at home I was going to send one. Lily came down for me to go to school, we like it better every time we go, however Mrs Sarcen did not take the class it was a Miss Pettifor. I quite thought G. would meet me out as he was working till eight and I do not think he went to the school. I should have thought better of him if he had come.

Wednesday November 7th

Eliza has asked me to go up town with her to buy Arthur a present as it is his birthday today. While we were looking in a shop window he passed, Eliza was in a "stew" she felt quite sure he saw us and he knew what we were looking for, she has bought an inkstand, paper knife and card. Elly has been cool with me this last day or two, I do not know why she should be so, but I shall let her come round. George was quiet again when he first came in, I shall have to know the reason, we did not go out. When we got in the parlour he asked me if I knew anything about 41 Friars Causeway, it seems I had got the wrong address, he thanked me for the card, I told him I thought he might think was forward for sending it. I would not own to it for some time, he asked me if I was ashamed of it. He is going to meet me tomorrow night.

Thursday November 8th

Eliza tells me Arthur did see us yesterday dinnertime and he did feel awkward as he suspected she was going to buy something, he likes his present very much. I forgotten to write yesterday George thought I kept out of his way on Tuesday dinnertime, I could not deny that. I went to see Mrs Barret altho' it rained very fast, she was very busy with the fancy work, the baby is a fat child and it is only six months old, I fancy somehow she is not very happy, but she may be and it is only my fancy. G. came to meet me, when we got home he asked me what was the matter with me last night as I seemed dull and unhappy, that gave me a chance to tell him about being quiet, he said he did not know to it and he is glad that I told him about it as he wished us to understand each other. He told me he thought I was afraid to tell him about different things. I did not tell him about Arthur's Birthday till to night, he thought I was not going to tell him.

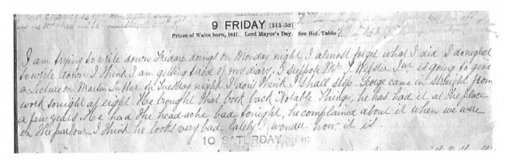

Friday November 9th

I am trying to write down Friday's doings on Monday night, I almost forgot what I did, I do neglect to write down, I think I am getting tired of my diary. I suppose Mr T. Webster Jun. is going to give a lecture on Martin Luther on Tuesday night,* I don't think I shall stop. George came in straight from work tonight at eight, he brought that book back "Notable Things", he has had it at the place a few years. He had the headache bad tonight, he complained about it when we were in the parlour, I think he looks very bad lately, I wonder how it is.

Saturday November 10th

I have had my felt hat altered after a deal of bother but it only cost me eight pence, I went out with Mother this afternoon to get the trimmings for it. We called at Mrs Baker's, John has not come over yet, I think I should give him the sack if I was Annie. I went to the Lecture Room, it was by a Mr Dolphin on Martin Luther, it was rather drier than some of his lectures I have heard there. George met me in Wellington Street, he had been round with his club money, he was rather chatty. He was telling me how much money he got 33 shillings I understood him to say, I was not to tell anyone as he only told very particular friends, so there is my orders. I got so wet he would have me change my dress when we got home. Mother was ill after she had her supper, she frightened me, I think she had something that did not agree with her.

Sunday November 11th

It was my turn at home this morning, I persuaded Mother to go out for a short time so she went. I went to school, A. and Mrs. Baker met me out and we had a walk, I met Mother she had been to hear Mr Hopps. George was down when we got home, he had met Eliza. Fancy, I took G. a little way to church, he said it was not the rule but that did not matter. We had a nice walk afterwards, he said he would have gone to Margaret's Church but I did not ask him, I wish he would go as I think he was nice most of the day, but I offended him at night by repeating what P. Poynor said that there was not any nice young men in that choir.

Monday November 12th

How cold it is this morning, I feel very loth to leave my bed, I suppose I shall have to. My eyes have been bad for two or three days, they are getting worse, I have bathed them in cold water, that does not seem to do them any good. I met George this dinnertime with Mr Staples, he was rather confused I thought, I do not know whether he intended to stop me but I walked on. He was late again tonight, we could not go out as it was so foggy, I was teasing him a bit, he tried to make me pick up a bill as I snatched out of his hand. He asked me if I would like to see "Patience", I do not care to go very much. Mrs Moore called in, her little girl is getting on nicely, she took her hair down in front of George, I should not have liked to have done it. I think she is a little bit vain.

Tuesday November 13th

I met George this dinnertime, he said I was not so early this dinnertime as I was last Tuesday. The steam stopped before seven, they were getting ready to hear this lecture, I came away with Eliza. G. passed us while we were talking, I thought he might have stopped, Eliza says she has often felt vexed at Arthur doing like that. Lily came down for me to go to the Grammar class, she told me some sad news about Mr Casely Snr., a letter came from London to say he would not live twenty four hours and she heard last

Friday that he was dead. It will come very hard on John now as they will have to leave their house and perhaps live in lodgings. She gave Flo' a lecture because she was a long time writing back.

Wednesday November 14th

Father went to see "Patience" tonight, he said it was very good. George came in straight from work at eight o'clock, I like him for that, he washed himself at our house. We had a walk, he brought up that affair again about the choir, he did not like the way I told him about it. He asked if I was disappointed as we did not go to see "Patience". We did not get on very well while we were talking, he was talking about going to hear "The Christy Minstrels" on Saturday night. I don't like to go because of the money so I talked about the "Livermore Brothers" that came of Fair week, so he said he was not talking about them, I told him I knew that, I did feel rather vexed about it. When he was going away he "blessed me", that is the first time since I was ill, I wonder if I was more loving, I did like him.

Thursday November 15th

P. Poyner was ill at work this afternoon, I think it was a fit that she had, I never want to see such a sight again, it frightened me so I nearly fainted. Elly came and spoke to me then I burst out crying, I felt better after that, it made us all quiet for the rest of the night, we had to go home early because the steam stopped. About half past six it seems George peeped thro' the letter box. I thought he had left off at six to go to the Vicar's Tea. Mrs Moore came and sat with us, I have done a lot to Father's shirt, G. called just before ten, he said to see how my cold was, I had almost given him up as it was so late. He had enjoyed himself in a quiet sort of way, I thought he looked very nice, he had on a navy blue suit.

Friday November 16th

I suppose P. Poyner is not very well, I am afraid it will take her some time to recover. I have not done so well at work this week, some of the smoking caps are rather bad work. George came in at eight, I was cleaning the window, we had a bit of fun over a wax candle, I threw it across the house and broken it in two. Of course, he ran me round the table and very soon caught me, then he tried to rub my face with it. He gilded the brackets belonging to the long blinds, I think they look much better now. I think he still looks bad, he has got a bit of a cold, I ask him if he has caught it off me. Every night we go in the parlour he puts a shawl round me, that does make me like him .

Saturday November 17th

It poured with rain at one o'clock, I should have been wet thro' if it had not been for George, he left my mackintosh and umbrella at the lodge bless him, how thoughtful it is of him, he does many acts of kindness for me and I do not return it enough, I will try to though. I went out with Lily this afternoon to buy a nightdress bag, I went to hear Mr Poynser lecture on "Flame", G. met me out, he seemed in high spirits, he asked me to get a bottle of Quinine Wine for him while he went into another shop and as I was going across the London Road I met K. Staples. When we got home he had bought such a nice pair of fur lined gloves and another pair for himself of course. I thanked him for them, he said I was quite welcome. He gave me a tiny looking glass and a bit of paper with some reading on, I shall always keep that, he did so many things to make me love him today.

Town Hall Square, showing the new Town Hall, opened in 1876.
(From Read R., Modern Leicester 1881)

Sunday November 18th

I went to Friar Lane Chapel* this morning with L. Cooper, I went to school in the afternoon. G. came to tea, he was very fussy and attentive, he asked me what church I was going to, I told him St. Margaret's then I asked him where he was going, he said to his own he thought. A short time after I asked him if he would like to go with me, he thanked me and declined this time but he would go some other time if I did not mind. He will go the next time I ask him I know, I did feel vexed and quiet about it. He met me out of church and we had a walk, I asked him another question about A. Staples, he would not answer it because I did not satisfy him about their choir, there he vexed me again.

Monday November 19th

Eliza has been telling me that her and Arthur had another row last night again, they have made it up and I suppose it is sweeter than ever. I am going to try and be amiable tonight and see if that will bring George out, because I feel I want to know if he cares for me, I fancy he does not sometimes.

He came about eight thirty and very agreeable he was at first, Mother went out soon after. It was about nine thirty before we went for our walk, I thought he was very quiet while we were out but he had got the toothache, I could excuse him then. That went off, he was still quiet, then I thought I would give over talking. He asked me if I was happy when we were in the parlour, I told him sometimes, O' I wish I could open my mind to him about a few things I am thinking about.

Tuesday November 20th

Lucy is still on the embroidery machine, we have some rare fun sometimes, she is such a lively girl. I heard some news about P. Dew's father, he fell down in a fit and he was brought home dead, what a shock that would be to the family. Lily came down for me and we went to school, Father often teases me about the penny Grammar class, well I do not mind about that as we learn something through going. We are bad girls because we do not stay for prayers, we shall have to stay as it looks rather mean to sneak out as we do. I am going to tea on Sunday to Lily's if nothing happens, she asked me to go last Sunday but I would not promise.

Wednesday November 21st

George came about 8.30, he has got such a bad cold, when I knew that I thought we had better not go out. He joined the St. John's Ambulance Society last night, I think it will be very instructive to him, he was showing us how to bandage anybody when they sprain themselves, Mother went in to Mrs Moore's for a short time. George thought I was quiet, he asked me if I was happy, I told him sometimes. He was trying to teach me how to play whist, I don't think I shall ever learn, as the trumps unsettle me so I feel inclined to laugh.

Thursday November 22nd

George came in straight from work, that just suits me but I would not let him know, he came in to paint the living room wall, I think his cold is a little better. I did a lot of machining for Mother, Father's second shirt is finished, that is another load off my mind, now I must begin to do my sewing for myself. I am afraid we are getting short of work now as the cutters out are leaving off at five o'clock, well we must expect that now, we have kept on full time longer than we usually do. G. told me he thought I was dull tonight, I am in it again.

Friday November 23rd

I have told George that Lily has asked me to go to tea on Sunday and he says he will let me go, I tell him he is good and I told him S. A. Staples is going to be married, Kate told me about it some weeks ago but she told me not to say anything. There are so many people tell me how bad I look , Father said B. Cooke asked him if I was ill again, I feel pretty well on the whole. I thought George was very nice tonight, I did like him, he asked me if I would go and see "Iolanthe" next week. I told him Father said I must save my coppers and go, he made no reply to that. He wondered if Eliza and Arthur would like to go, so I shall ask Eliza, I hardly think they will go so soon.

Saturday November 24th

I stayed at home this afternoon and did my work, I went to hear the lecture on "Hiawatha" by Rev. P. Hopper and I thought it was an excllent lecture. George was rather late or we came out early, I began to feel vexed and wonder if he would come. I think he noticed me being vexed because he said he was sorry he was late. I told George what Father said about me not asking his consent to let me go out with George. I told him I left that for George to do, he said he would ask him. George was glad I told him as he would be ready for Father when he said anything about it. We are to walk out more often as George thinks it will be better for both of us.

Sunday November 25th

It was my turn at home this morning, we get up so late on Sunday morning it throws me so backwards with the dinner. There was a children's service at the church this afternoon, Mr Odell addressed them, I suppose it was the first time, I think he was very good. I went to Mrs Small's for tea, Miss Houghton was there again, she generally is when I go. We went to Christ Church and I met G. afterwards, I suppose A. Baker came down to our church and was looking for me, I am so sorry I was not there, because I think Annie is so lonely now.

Monday November 26th

There is a tea at Christ Church today, Lily asked me to go but I did not care to, then she asked me to go to the entertainment afterwards, I don't think I shall go. Everybody is telling me how ill I look, if I am told it much longer I shall feel ill, they say I have got such a white face. P. Poynor has come back today, she is a great deal better. I thought George was rather late, he brought the copper lid for Mother, he promised it some time back and it is done at last. We had a walk I enjoyed it, G. would like me to go to his church some Friday night to hear the lessons explained by the Vicar for the following Sunday. He asked me how I should like to hear the Alpine Choir. I should like to tell him about paying for myself, but I do not know how to start.

Tuesday November 27th

I have been told two or three times again today how bad I look, Father and George told me about it last night, O' dear, what shall I do, G. says go to bed earlier. The embroidery is finished today, I am pleased as I wanted a change, I like my little sewing machine. P. Dilley when she came back from dinner told me that she had seen my young man and he did laugh. Lily came early for me tonight, she was at our house when I got home from work. We went to school, I am sure Mrs Sarcen teaches me a few things I did not know, we stayed for prayers tonight. Lily and I are going to Belgrave Church on Sunday morning, weather permitting.

Wednesday November 28th

I have got the "Girls Own Paper" for December, I think there is some very good advice in it, how to be happy, healthy and wise etc.. I met George at two o'clock, he asked me if I would go to see "Iolanthe" tonight, I said I did not know, he came in straight from work. I did think I was going with Father and he would come to us, then I could have payed for myself, but I was deceived again. I must try somehow to give George the money, but I feel rather afraid of beginning about it. I do not like the idea of him paying for me. I was very pleased with the Opera and enjoyed it very much. George had the toothache while we were there, I was ever so sorry for him. I think I shown my fondness for him so much, I feel vexed that he should think I cared for him too much.

Thursday November 29th

Elly was telling me this morning that Arthur had said there is to be a club meeting a week next Monday night and he asked her if she would let him off for that night, he said that George would try to go. George has not said anything to me yet, he need not talk about me being close about different things for I am sure he is. I went round with Eliza tonight at seven and who should we meet in Sanvey Gate but George, I think he half stopped then he walked on. He might have spoken to me, perhaps he did not care to, he has gone to a meeting at the school tonight, so I did not see him, I have been quite busy.

Friday November 30th

I suppose P. Poynor had another fit last night, she is having them oftener than she used to. I don't think she looked right when she came back to work altho' she said she was better. George was here when I got home tonight, his face is swelled but it has not stopped aching. He was very quiet and I thought nasty tempered, I got quite disgusted with him once or twice. I know I ought not to have been as it is an aggravating pain, I was very sorry after he had gone away. I told him not to come and meet me tomorrow night if his face was not any better, I think he was vexed about it.

December

Saturday December 1st

George's business premises on St. Saviour's Road
in the early 20th Century.

I have got more money this week than I have ever got in my life, 13s8d only fancy, I must not get too much or I will have my work docked. Father tells me George's face is not any better and he is going to get somebody to go round with the club money. I went out with Mother and Father this afternoon, then we called at Mrs Baker's, Annie says John has been over, his business has kept him from coming over before. I felt very unhappy about George and sorry I was not more amiable with him last night. I went to hear the lecture on "Wandering in the Sunny South" by Mr Stafford, it was after nine when we came out, I could not see G. anywhere about, he was not at our house when I got home. I wonder if he is worse or if I have offended him, if I did but know, the suspense is dreadful.

Sunday December 2nd

Father decided on going to enquire how George is, his face has swollen very much. He told Father to ask me to go round sometime this morning. I promised Lily I would go to church if the weather was fine but it looks like rain and I should like to see George, so I decided to go. He said he was glad to see me and he called Mrs Grace in to introduce us to each other. I am going to meet him when I come from school, he is coming down to tea. I stayed in with him at night, he blessed me for that and he called me "my dear" several times and asked me if I could love anyone better than him. He said he loved me better than anybody, I am so very happy, he has not been like this before, how it makes me love him, he has been so very nice today.

Monday December 3rd

There is another order for smoking caps come in, I am so glad as there is not much of the other work about, P. Poyner has come back to work again, the doctor says she may have fits for some time now, I think it is very hard for her. George was at our house when I got home from work at seven, his face is much better again today, I am so pleased. He shown me a letter from his brother and another from his sister, both of them sent invitations for us to go over sometime, I am sure it is very kind of them. G. would like to go home for the New Year, he was very nice again tonight, I was telling him about the money I earned, he tells me I do well. I had his coat to mend again and he said it would do nicely, there is a feather in my cap, he went home rather early.

Tuesday December 4th

Lily came down for me and we went to school, I thought she was rather vexed as I did not go down for her last Sunday morning, I told her how it was. George was at our house when I got home, he told me last night that he should come and do some painting. I am still happy and lively, it is so much nicer to be happy, I wonder how long it will last. We are going a walk tomorrow night if it is fine. I feel as though I want a walk, it is good for my health and I soon miss my walk.

Wednesday December 5th

The girls in our room are going on short time, Miss Ross came just before five o'clock to tell Lucy and I to stop as the smoking caps are wanted. When I got home Mother made me have some supper as I did not take my tea, G. was here at seven painting, we did have a lark, I felt just in the humour for it. Afterwards we had a walk and he asked me if I would go home with him for the New Year, I think I shall go if nothing happens. The reason he does not show me his Mother's letters is because she does not write very well.

Thursday December 6th

I went straight from work to show Lily how to do some crewel work, I was surprised to find her ill, I was so sorry for her she was in such pain, it must be bad for her, she so often has there bilious attacks now. George came down earlier than I expected him, he told me I looked serious, I was thinking about Lily. He is beginning to put his hand on my shoulder when Mother is about, I feel so silly and try to get out of reach. We had a very nice walk again, I pushed him in a ditch, then he sent me in one, I am still larking and happy; for how long!

Friday December 7th

We went to hear "The ALPINE CHOIR", Mother and Father went as well, we got a seat behind Eliza and Arthur, Mrs Cooper and Ada, I enjoyed the music. Father liked it better than I thought he would, I was rather vexed at G.. He sat such a long way from me all the time we were in the Hall and I could see Arthur paying the greatest attention to Eliza. I was rather quiet when we got home, I think he noticed it because when we were in the parlour he asked me what was the matter with me, of course I said nothing. He went away ever so funny, I was so sorry afterwards.

Saturday December 8th

A party of six went to Oadby this afternoon, I think we all enjoyed ourselves. When I was going for Eliza I met G., he was quiet and did not say much, that made me rather dull. I have bought a tobacco pouch for Father's birthday, I am going to crewel work it. We had our tea in the coffee house when we came back from Oadby, I went to the lecture by Rev. J. Wood on "Pepys' Diary", it was different to what I expected, all about school boards, it might be interesting to some people but not to me. G. met me, he had not finished taking his money round, so I went with him, we got along very well, he took my arm on the London Road, he did not do that last night, perhaps it was because Mother and Father was with us.

Sunday December 9th

We did get up late this morning and I have got to stay at home, I had hard work to get done. There was not much fire when Father got home and he began to jaw me dreadfully, of course I answered him back, that did not suit. I could not eat any dinner, it would have choked me, then he said it was my nasty temper, I had a good cry. I went to school, G. came to tea, he asked me to go to his church so I went, the vicar preached on "Thy Will Be Done", we came straight home at night because it rained. Mother went out for a short time so that left us alone. I told G. about Father, he thought there was something the matter with me because I was so quiet.

Monday December 10th

George was asking me last night if he had done anything to offend me, so after a great deal of persuading I told him I thought he was getting tired of me. He asked if it was because he sat such a long way from me, he did that so as Mother could see better and he thought I was indifferent towards him. I told him I thought I ought to pay for myself when we go to places of amusement, he said it was absurd of me to think of such a thing. He was very nice to me when he came down tonight, we were going out but it rained again. Mother went of an errand so we were alone, I told him last night if ever he did get tired of me I should want him to tell me, he says he never shall get tired if I am willing for him to care for me, (I am sure I am).

Tuesday December 11th

I left off work at five last night, but tonight all in our room have got to work till seven, I should think we are getting busy again. Lily came down for me and we went to school, I was surprised to hear that she has had a letter from Mr Caseley, it is a very sad one, he feels his Father's death very much indeed and they have got to leave their house in January. Lily is much better, she would keep me talking all the night if I was not to make a push. I wrote the beginning of this on Tuesday night in my bedroom, I had to leave off in a hurry as Father called to me to turn the gas out, so I am finishing it on Friday dinnertime.

Wednesday December 12th

I met George this dinnertime, he gave me some brooches to look at, some as he had got from Ball's*. We are going to buy one for Mother, we chose one I think it is four shillings. I think it is very good of G. to think about Mother in that way, she will be very pleased with it I am sure. We went on the Belgrave Road and we saw a house that has been partly blown down by the wind last night, I am afraid it has done a great deal of damage. We were talking about A. Beck, he asked G. last night if he would ever get Elly to go to church with him, and he has told Elly he will be a teetotaller if she will go to church. G. thinks he is too free with strangers, I mean that he opens his mind too much.

Thursday December 13th

Elly asked me this morning if I was in trouble because I looked miserable, I do not feel very well. I am very happy only for that. George brings a great deal of happiness into my life, I think he is a very nice young man, he seems a constant lover. He came in straight from work and washed himself at our house, then we went to hear a lecture at the Temperance Hall by Mr D. on "Plants and how they prey upon Animals". It was a science lecture of course and very good too, it reminded me of those lectures at the beginning of the year, there is a slight difference in my life since then.

Friday December 14th

There is another gross of smoking caps ordered, we are quite busy. Mrs Short was telling me she did not think we should get all the work done by Christmas, we are generally short at this time of the year. Father

Premises occupied by Rowe & Sons, Printers and Stationers, in Belvoir St., later in the 19th Century *(Mr G. Peck) went to a sale last night and bid for a set of jugs, they were knocked down to him so I had to go with him for them tonight and when we got to the sale room they were gone, I was not sorry because we want other things before them. I began to crewel work that tobacco pouch, I shall not buy another it splits every time I put the needle through. G. came about 9.30.*

Saturday December 15th

I called at Lily's this afternoon to take some underlinen back as she had lent me, she enjoyed herself at the wedding on Thursday in a quiet sort of way. She is going to London at Christmas and she has answered Mr Caseley's letter. I afterwards went out with Mother and Father, he was looking at some tea services, Mother turned awkward and left us. Father made me a present of a pair of slippers, G. says I am very fortunate in having such a Father. I went to the Lecture Room, it was a sort of musical evening, I enjoyed it very much. It was twenty past nine when I came out, G. had been waiting some time for me. One young fellow is dead, that is a member of the Oddfellows Club, they want George to be a bearer, he is only three and twenty.

Sunday December 16th

We still keep nagging at it, I hate so much discord, it makes home so miserable. It is Mother's birthday, I put the brooch in her cocoa tin so she found it this morning and she says somebody thinks about her, I think Father will buy a tea service. I had a walk with Father this morning, school this afternoon and I came straight home. G. came to tea, he asked me to go to his church but I preferred to go to my own, he has proposed to go to St. Margaret's on Christmas Day.

Monday December 17th

We are working till eight tonight, it does make me tired. Mrs Moore was at our house when I got home, she told me something that made me feel dull. It was about G., A. Measures and another girl had been talking about him being so very fond of Emma, they seemed to speak as though he could not care much for me. They said he used to sit with her till it was time for him to go into the vestry when she used to go to church with him. I felt so funny towards him when he came in, when he was going away he asked me what was the matter with me as I kept turning away from him so funny. He wanted to come in tomorrow night, I think he asked me if I should have anything to do, I told him I dare say I should. He would have liked me to have gone up the station with him tomorrow dinnertime.

Tuesday December 18th

Mrs Beecroft (his brother's wife) came through Leicester by the twelve train, G. asked me to go to the station with him, but I fancied he only asked me as a matter of course, so I would not go. I met him at dinnertime, G.'s sister in law thought I should be there, a cousin was at the station, she given him an invitation for Christmas. G. did not say whether he would come in tonight, I sent word to Lily as I could not go to school, she is coming down before she goes to London. When I got home G. was here and I heard some sad news about Father, J. Kirk has been fighting him this afternoon, I think it seems so disgraceful. G. was helping chop the mincemeat, then we went for some brandy for Mother, afterwards we saw Father and came home with him.

Wednesday December 19th

We left off at seven tonight, we have soon done the work up, I am not sorry as I have plenty of work to do at home. G. came in at eight o'clock, he was rather surprised to see me at home, I told him I thought he did not want me to go with him yesterday morning, he said he thought I was too busy to go and he perhaps did wrong in considering that but he would have liked me to go. I told him about the last time he went home as how I thought he did not care for me to go with him. I do not think he cares for me a little bit, I am so miserable.

Thursday December 20th

I came home before seven tonight so I went with Mother and Mrs Moore to the tea shop, we had a pair of decanters with the cheques. I have got so much to do before Christmas, I do not know what to do first. I met Lily when I was coming home, she had been down to our house to see me before she went to London, what a thoughtful girl she is. She sent the compliments of the season to Mother and Father and G., she is in high spirits, I think she would have been disappointed if she had not gone to London. George came in about eight, he afterwards went to the practice and he asked me to meet him out, of course I could not refuse, I bet he thinks he can soon get round me.

Friday December 21st

We are having all the bits to do up at work, I shall not care how soon I get away, it does not pay me to stop. I left off about five but Miss Ross asked me to call in tomorrow morning. I went up town and got a few things in, then I went home and made some mincepies and cakes. George came, I did some work, I am so very happy tonight. We had a goose sent us for a Xmas box, Mother and I left our presents for Father on the table so that he might find them in the morning. George has bought a cigar case for him, I was surprised when he told me about it. He says he has been here a good deal lately and Father has always been good to him, I am glad.

Saturday December 22nd

I called at the place about ten but there was not anything to do. Eliza was just going away so we went up town and bought some lace for our necks, then I went home and finished my cleaning. I had to go poking for my money at one, G. went as far as our place with me. I went out with Mother and Father this afternoon, Father bought a tea service for Mother, when we left him we went round Jacob's Bazaar*, there were some *nice things there. I went to meet G. at eight, afterwards he went into Brandon Street to pay a club and I should think he was half an hour gone, I did feel vexed. I thought of what A. Measures said that how he would not stay many minutes at their home because Emma was waiting for him, so I was very quiet when he came, he was chattering away, he could see there was something the matter with me. He wanted to know what was the matter with me but I would not tell him.*

Sunday December 23rd

It is my turn at home this morning but Mother did not go out, I do feel miserable, I should like to tell George what I think about his going on last night but I do not know how to begin. We went into church for an address on missionary work in India, I was interested. Mother and I had a walk, after we saw G. but I would not stop. When he came down he told us he had been home to write a letter, he said I ought to have stopped for him, I told him I thought he would not want me. I went church with him and we had a walk afterwards, he said he thought of asking me to meet him out of school some Sunday and have a walk.

Monday December 24th

I finished my cleaning this morning, Mother was cleaning the goose, it was a nasty job. P. Poyner came down this afternoon for her music. Mother thinks she is such a pretty girl, she sang a few songs afterwards. Mother and I went out, I do not feel very well today, I have such a pain in my side. I feel afraid of another illness so I must take care of myself. George came down for me and we went to hear the "Messiah", he had to stand up all the night, that made it very awkward. We passed A. Staples and Mr Baker in Church Gate, I felt rather confused, neither of us said anything about it. I wonder what George thought, I fancy he is not happy with me as he used to be with Emma, I should like to know.

Tuesday December 25th

I had to stay at home and help Mother cook the dinner, I had a very nice card from Lily and a letter, George sent me two cards and he gave me an ancient and modern hymn book of tunes last night for a Xmas box, he is always buying something for me I tell him, he laughed at me for talking like that. He came for dinner, I should have liked to have gone for a walk in the afternoon, he did ask me but I thought indifferently so I did not answer decidedly. He went to church with me for the first time, the choir sung some carols. G. tells me I am not fond of kissing he thinks, and he thought I did not care for those cards as I hardly thanked him for them, he little thinks what a lot I think about them and him as well.

Wednesday December 26th

Eliza and Arthur called round this morning, she asked me to go on Friday afternoon instead of Thursday as she had asked me, I do not mind at all as I can do with the time at home. G. stayed to talk with me this dinnertime, he saw me through the window, I was writing my adventures down here. He wants to see my diary so bad, I tell him he is asking too much. I met him about 4. 30 and we went to Mr Lanks', I was introduced to two Miss

Advertisement 1881 for
"Sensible Christmas Presents"
(From Read R., Modern Leicester 1881)

Johnsons, Mr Knight and Mr Dobson, I enjoyed myself very much considering it was a strange place. We had a few games of cards, it was after twelve when we came away. Mr Lanks asked me to go again soon, they are homely people.

Thursday December 27th

Eliza promised to come down for me this morning to have a walk but she was not very well so she sent Lucy. George and Mr Cross came in and had a mincepie and some wine, we had a bit of singing then. G. thought I was in the parlour alone, he was just deceived. Lucy had a walk with me then I went home and had some pheasant for dinner. G. called about two, I thought he was rather quiet. In the afternoon I had a nice walk with Mother and Father, then we called at Mrs Baker's, Annie says she spent a very quiet Xmas. It was nine before G. came in tonight and he was so quiet. I think there must be something the matter with him, he went away so very funny. When he had gone I made a start at weeping, then thought I would not.

Friday December 28th

I stayed at home and did some cleaning this morning, I have not been so happy this Xmas as I thought I should be, perhaps I have been building too many castles in the air. I went out shopping with Eliza this afternoon, I bought a tie to send to George for the New Year. I had tea at Mrs Cooper's, Arthur came down about eight, I came away soon after, they have spent a quiet Xmas. George came about nine, he was rather independent I thought at first, but when he had been in a little time he got all right. He said he hoped I should enjoy myself, I am so happy now.

Saturday December 29th

I have written a letter to Lily and sent her a card, then I got ready to go into the country, George came in for his bag soon after eleven. Father and Mother went up to the station with me, G. had no time to come with me. G.'s brother met us at the station, we stayed at Market Overton* for a short time then we went on to Witham. I went through a great deal of introduction. The heartiest welcome I had was from G.'s mother, she came and kissed me directly before I could introduce myself, I did not feel *half so strange as I thought I should. They soon made me at home, I slept with Mrs J. Beecroft, her husband came in the bedroom and G. followed, I was surprised at him kissing me before them.*

Sunday December 30th

George and I went to church and three of the children went with us, the parson only gobbled the prayers over. After dinner Mrs Exton came, I do think she is like Kate, we went to church in the afternoon, John was a bad boy, he is a regular tartar, I was so happy. George and I was looking through the family bible, I think he is so much nicer at home, it did make me like him. There were more of his friends came for tea, Miss Waterfield, a cousin of G.'s was there, I did not care for her very much at first but I got to like her better, we had a sing at night, I am happy. The children kept letting things out, I saw Emma's photo', George shown it to me and little Annie told me two or three times who she was.

Monday December 31st

I was nursing babies most of the time I was there and I like it very well. I was rather took back once or twice, Mrs Beecroft kept forgetting and calling me Emma, I hardly liked that but I don't suppose she could help it for she begged my pardon. We went to the station with them this morning, I had an invitation to Burton at Easter, I think we are going if nothing happens. George and I drove home alone, he asked me if I had enjoyed myself and all the rest of my thoughts, we got home about two. (I have soon begun to call it home, I fancy I did so to George). A young lady came to see them, Miss Towell, she seemed to have more to say to George than I cared about and I wondered the reason. It seems as she is the first girl he went out with, she gave him up so G. tells me and she has had a good few young fellows, she has just parted with one. At night we went to G.'s sister's to a party, we did not get home till three on New Year's morning. We began the Year with card playing, rather a bad start. George's cousin told me she hoped she would have the pleasure of seeing me again sometime.

Tuesday January 1st 1884

We started from Witham about ten this morning, Mrs Exton invited me over to Osgodby, * G. promised her we would go at Whitsuntide if nothing happened. We got home about two, they seemed pleased to see us, Father said he was glad I had behaved myself, I am sure I enjoyed myself better than ever I thought I should. I have not time to keep a diary this year as I have something else to do. I have a happier year before me this year than I had last by all appearances. George came into my bedroom this morning and gave me two such nice cards, the verses have quite taken my fancy, I do think a lot of them. George was pleased with his tie and he thanked me many times for it, I told him more than it was worth.

Postscript

The diary contains a handful of other entries marking subsequent important occasions in Ada's life.

George and Ada with
their eldest son, Harold.

March 19th 1884

I have cause to remember my twenty first birthday for many a long day. George given me an engagement ring and he mentioned marriage to me for the first time.

I was surprised because I did not expect it, he thought Easter time /85, but afterwards he preferred Christmas /84. I shall try my best to make him very very happy, I should miss him now if we were to part.

June 18th 1884

I was confirmed by Bishop Mitchinson, his address was on "The Sower and the Seed", another happy day for me. George talked so sensible and nice when we got home after the service. Mrs Moore called in, she told Mother she thought we were very fond of each other.

December 29th 1884

A wonderful happy happy day for me (Our Wedding Day). I did enjoy myself and my husband was attentive. I compared my lot with poor Clara Underwood's and could see the difference between the two young men. I do not think I shall have cause to repent of my choice, and how strange for me to have the one I have loved so long back. I little thought of this when I used to meet George as I went backwards and forwards to school, Oh, how I love him.

Ada and George were married at St. Margaret's Church, Leicester, by the Rev. Odell. Ada was 21 and George 27 years of age. At first they lived at 9 Pares Street with Ada's parents, but had moved a short distance to 9 Burgess Street by the time their first child, Harold Jackson Beecroft (Mrs Blow's father), was born on 25 October 1885.

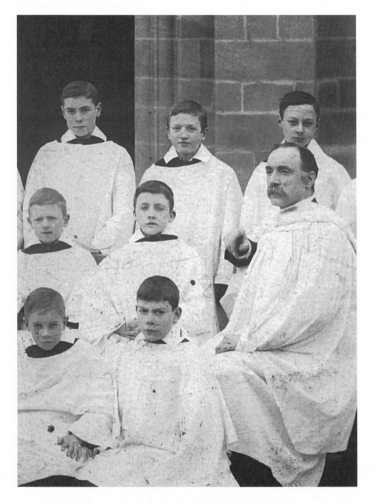

Ada and George's eldest son Harold (Back row, centre) in the choir of St. Martin's Church, Leicester.

October 25th 1885

Our boy was born at five minutes to twelve at night (Sunday). Oh, I was so pleased when it was all over. It seems so strange for me to be a Mother, I should not like to part with him for any money now.

A family outing to Mablethorpe. Ada is in the centre of the back seat.

Two more children were born over the next two years, Percy, and Alice May - commonly known as Dot - who died of diphtheria on 29 October 1892 at the age of three.

Ada and George's eldest sons, Harold (aged two and a half) and Percy (aged one)

May 13th 1887

Another son was born to us, I seem to have two babies now, but I suppose I shall pull through somehow. But I should not like to part with him for any money now, he gets on capital and is such a good boy.

July 17th 1889

We have a daughter this time for a change and we are very pleased with her, she is such a good girl so far. I should not care to part with her but have got as many as I want and can manage for the present.

A fourth child, George Cecil, was born in 1892. He died on 26 February 1916 at the age of 23.

ABOVE: Ada and George with
their grandson, Harold.

LEFT: Ada holding Mrs. Blow as a baby.
Also in the picture are Mr. Mott (Harold's father-
in-law) and Mrs. Blow's mother, both standing, and
Ada's father (seated). The boy at the front is
Harold Louis Beecroft, Mrs. Blow's brother.

In 1895 the family moved to 49 East Bond Street, and in 1900 to 6 St. Saviour's
Road, where George established his own business as a joiner, builder and
undertaker. Ada Beecroft died on 22 October 1925, at the age of 62 years.
George Beecroft outlived her by almost nine years, dying on 1 February 1934 at
the age of 76.

KEY

1 and **2** Ada's Parents. **3** Ada's youngest son, Cecil (died age 23 in 1916). **4** Ada's second son, Percy. **5** George. **6** Ada. **7** Mrs Blow's Mother, Martha. **8** Ada's eldest son Harold (Mrs Blow's father).

The wedding on 11th October 1915 of Ada and George's eldest son Harold Jackson Beecroft to Martha Evelyn Mary Mott.

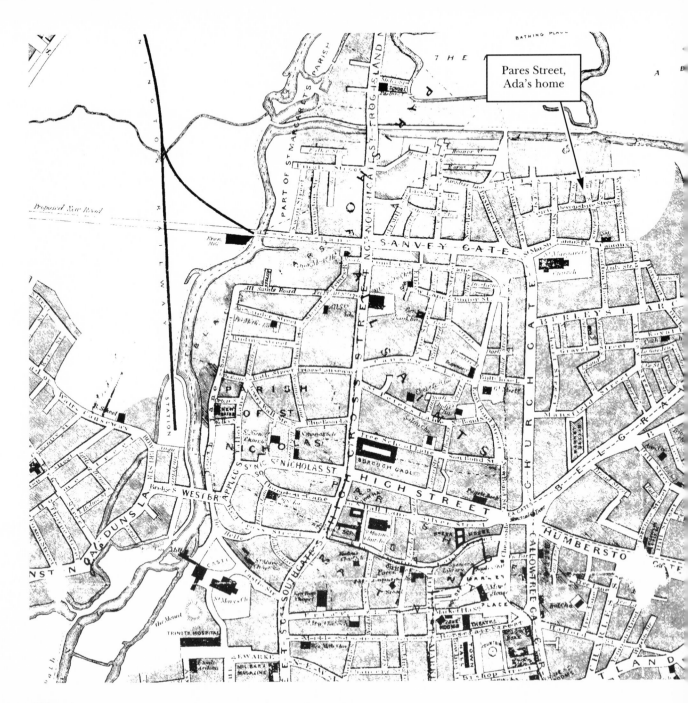

Pares Street,
Ada's home

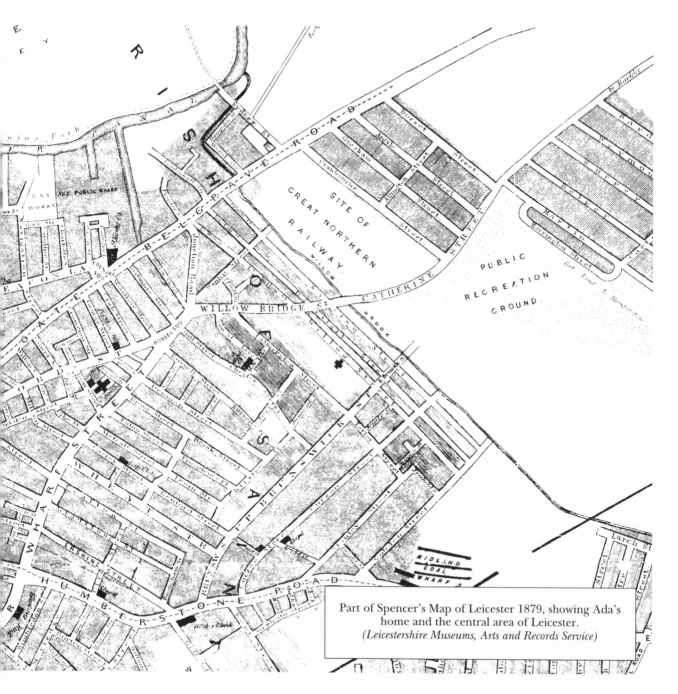

Part of Spencer's Map of Leicester 1879, showing Ada's home and the central area of Leicester.
(Leicestershire Museums, Arts and Records Service)

NOTES ON THE TEXT

1 Jan **Miss E. Cooper**: Ada's friend Eliza.

Mrs Twigger was a friend of the Jackson family

3 Jan **dollying**: a dolly was a wooden implement used in washing clothes.
Miss L. Small was Ada's friend Lily.

The **Oadby Road** was the London Road, leading to the village of Oadby, about four miles from Leicester

4 Jan **Elly**: Ada' s closest friend.

Mrs Biggs was Elly's landlady.

Annie B. was Ada's friend Annie Baker.

The **Museum** refers to New Walk Museum, originally a school for Nonconformists, designed by Joseph Hansom and opened in 1837. The building was opened as a museum in 1849 by the Borough Council. So popular was its winter programme of free Saturday lectures that a purpose-built Lecture Hall was added to the Museum in the 1870s.

5 Jan **Miss Ross**: the forewoman in Ada's department at Thomas Webster and Co..

"I must practise more" is a reference to playing the piano

6 Jan **the Course**: the Racecourse, now Victoria Park. The Races were held there from the early 19th century until July 1883. In the following year they moved to the new racecourse at Oadby.

The **Common** was Freemen's Common, covering around 78 acres of land between Welford Road and Aylestone Road.

The **Temperance Hall** in Granby Street was built for Thomas Cook in 1853. It was the only hall of any size in Leicester until the De Montfort Hall was built in 1913, and hosted concerts, political meetings and other large gatherings, as well as lectures. It was demolished in 1961.

7 Jan **"school in the afternoon"**: i.e. an adult class at St. Margaret's Church School. Ada was a regular worshipper at St. Margaret's Church.

Mrs Clayton was the wife of the vicar of St. Margaret's.

The **Rev. W.J. Lewis** was a curate at the church.

8 Jan The Monday lectures which Ada attended were held at the Temperance Hall.

See 6 Jan above.

11 Jan   **"Grandfather Hyde"**: Ada's maternal grandfather.

14 Jan   **Mr Clayton**: Rev. Lewis Clayton, Vicar of St. Margaret's, Leicester; Suffragan Bishop of Leicester 1903 and Asst. Bishop of Peterborough 1913

15 Jan   **Miss E. Small**: Lily's sister Ellen.

Kate was probably Kate Staples, whose sister **Emma** also features in the diary. An **Alice** Staples is also mentioned elsewhere.

16 Jan   **St. Margaret's School**: presumably St. Margaret's Girls' and Infants' School in Canning Place.

Ada's friend **Bella Cooke** is the Miss B. Cooke referred to elsewhere.

18 Jan   **A. Measures**: Addy Measures, who was employed at Ada's father's place of work

1 9 Jan   **the Park**: Abbey Park, Leicester's first municipal park, opened in 1882 by the Prince and Princess of Wales.

21 Jan   **Mr Odell**: a curate of St. Margaret's.

25 Jan   **Liberal Club**: in Gallowtree Gate at this time. A new Liberal Club designed by Edward Burgess was built in Bishop Street in 1888.

27 Jan   **the Granby**: the Granby Coffee and Cocoa House in Granby Street

30 Jan   **"the Factory"**: probably George and John Thomas Thorp, elastic web manufacturers of Friday Street, where George Beecroft had served his apprenticeship.

1 Feb   **ulster**: a long loose overcoat, often with a belt.

Mr Dale was Eliza's friend Arthur Dale

6 Feb   **battledore and shuttlecock**: game played with a small wooden raquet and shuttlecock

11 Feb   **Christ Church**: Bow Street, by Wharf Street, built in 1838-9, to cater for the increase of population in the north-east of the town. Closed 1956, and demolished the following year.

24 Feb   **Wardles**: milliners, of Burgess Street.

27 Feb   **the Union**: the Leicester Union Workhouse in Sparkenhoe Street, built in 1836 and enlarged in 1850. In its latter years it became Hillcrest Hospital for the elderly, and was demolished in 1977.

28 Feb   **"Mully Grubs"**: i.e. "mulligrubs", meaning depressed in spirits.

Emery's was a newsagent's shop in Belgrave Gate.

1 Mar   **Evington**: village about three miles from Leicester.

2 Mar   **"Patience"**: Gilbert and Sullivan operetta.

4 Mar   **St. Matthew's**: St. Matthew's Church, Leicester, large church in the Wharf Street area, built in 1865-67 to the design of George Gilbert Scott, and popularly known as the "Poor Man's Cathedral". George Beecroft was a regular attender here, and sang in the choir.

7 Mar   The Royal Opera House in **Silver Street** was built in 1876-7. The other theatre in Leicester at this time was the Theatre Royal in Horsefair Street, built in 1836. The Floral Hall in Belgrave Gate, opened in 1876, also staged concerts and theatrical performances.

14 Mar   **Library**: the Free Lending Library in Belvoir Street, opened in 1871.

15 Mar   **"I suppose he is going home at Easter"**: George's family lived at South Witham in Lincolnshire.

16 Mar   **Lucy Cooper**: Eliza's sister.

20 Mar   **Cook Memorial Hall**: the Annie Elizabeth Cook Memorial Hall in Archdeacon Lane, near to the Baptist Chapel where Thomas Cook worshipped. Built by him in 1882 in memory of his daughter, who died in 1880.

24 Mar   **"all made Donkeys"**: a reference to the card game Donkey, also known as Pig, where the last person to lay their cards on the table was the "Donkey".

25 Mar   **St. George's Church**: Rutland Street, Leicester. Built 1823- 7 to serve the expanding population of the town.

6 Apr   **Gallowtree Gate Chapel**: Congregationalist chapel in Chapel Yard, off Gallowtree Gate.

8 Apr   **Canning Place School Room**: St. Margaret's Girls' and Infants' School.

20 Apr   **Sunday Schools Industrial Exhibition**: annual exhibition of craft work by local Sunday Schools, usually held at the Floral Hall in Belgrave Gate. **Crewel work** consists of a design worked on linen or cloth with worsted yarn.

22 Apr   **Great Meeting Chapel**: Unitarian chapel in East Bond Street.

2 May   **"roar"**: to have a loud fit of crying.

12 May **the Fair**: the May Fair, granted by a charter of Edward IV in 1473, and held after 1752 for eight days from 12 May. Like the **October Fair** (see 10 Oct below), it was held in Humberstone Gate until 1904.

15 May **Belvoir Castle**: seat of the Duke of Rutland, 28 miles north-east of Leicester. The nearest railway station would be at Redmile, on the Great Northern and London line.

23 May **Gee's**: mourning warehouse, milliner and furrier of 51-55 Market Place. Later Gee Nephew and Co.

3 June **Iron Church**: St. Michael and All Angels, Melton Road, Leicester. A temporary church was built in 1878, and replaced by a permanent structure in 1885-7.

10 June **Harvey Lane Chapel**: large Baptist chapel on the site of what is now the Holiday Inn. Its former ministers included William Carey, the Indian missionary, and the great Baptist orator, Robert Hall.

30 June **Market House**: the Corn Exchange in Market Place, built 1851-6 to the design of F.W. Ordish.

5 July **Liberal Club**: see 25 Jan above.

6 July **Belgrave Wake Monday**: the village of Belgrave lay just beyond the eastern boundary of Leicester itself. The Belgrave Wake was a traditional holiday celebrated in early July, usually accompanied by a fair.

14 July **excursion to Skegness**: In 1883 the Great Northern Railway Company opened a branch line from Marefield Junction near Tilton to a station in Belgrave Road, Leicester, giving direct rail access to the East coast.

16 July **Horn's shop**: Carts Lane. Haberdashery, toys and fancy goods.

18 July **"polinase"**: i.e. polonaise, a woman's dress consisting of bodice with skirt open over a petticoat.

21 July **Albert**: watch-chain with crossbar, named after Queen Victoria's Consort, Prince Albert.

23 July **Bradgate Park**: around six miles from Leicester, and part of the estates of the Grey family at this time. Purchased in 1928 by Charles Bennion of Thurnby and given in trust to the people of the City and County of Leicester.

25 July **Staples**: Henry Staples, haberdasher of Highcross Street. The Kate and Emma Staples who feature in the diary were probably his daughters.

28 July **Fosse**: presumably the Fosse Road, on the western side of Leicester.

10 Aug **washing machine**: this probably consisted of a vertical machine with an agitator, operated by a handle or treadle.

11 Aug **wreath and fall**: circular headdress of interwoven material or flowers.

13 Aug **Mrs Grace's**: George's lodgings.

20 Aug **Kirby**: presumably Kirby Muxloe, a village around five miles from Leicester.

25 Aug **Mr Butler's**: probably Samuel Butler, a local retail chemist, well known later for his Sea Breeze salts.

26 Aug **English cholera**: summer and autumn illness causing diarrhoea and sickness. Not to be confused with the more serious and often fatal Asiatic or epidemic cholera.

7 Sept **New Walk**: pedestrian walk between the town centre and the Racecourse (now Victoria Park), laid out in 1785 and originally known as Queen's Walk.

12 Sept **Cross Market**: the Wednesday Market, held in Highcross Street from at least the 12th century. In 1884 it was moved to the site of the present Market (formerly the Saturday Market).

13 Sept **fire at Gascoine's**: probably Royce, Gascoine and Co., boot and shoe manufacturers of Highcross Street.

15 Sept **Coffee House**: probably Eastgates Coffee House, at the corner of Eastgates and Church Gate.

17 Sept **jerry**: chamber pot.

18 Sept **Scraptoft**: village around four miles from Leicester.

22 Sept **Enderby**: village around six miles from Leicester.

25 Sept **Birstall Lodge**: farm at Birstall, around three miles from Leicester.

4 Oct **Occupation Road**: now University Road.

5 Oct **Jacob's and Kennard's**: furnishing contractor of Horsefair Street.

6 Oct **Floral Hall**: see 7 Mar above.

8 Oct **Great Meeting**: See 22 Apr above.

11 Oct **the Fair**: the October Pleasure Fair, originally the Michaelmas Fair, granted by John of Gaunt in 1375, and held for nine days from 10 October in Humberstone Gate. (See also 12 May above).

16 Oct **St. Martin's School**: adult evening school, referred to elsewhere as the "penny grammar class", probably held at St. Martin's Girls' School in Union Street.

28 Oct **Oddfellows**: Friendly Society. There were branches of both the Manchester and Nottingham Unity of Oddfellows in Leicester at this time.

1 Nov the identity of the **"old sandman"** is not known.

Municipal elections were held in November at this time. **North St. Margaret's** was one of seven municipal wards in the town.

2 Nov **Free Press**: Midland Free Press, a weekly newspaper published in Leicester "in the Liberal interest".

9 Nov i.e. to mark the 400th anniversary of Luther's birth.

18 Nov **Friar Lane Chapel**: Baptist chapel.

12 Dec **Ball's**: jeweller and watchmaker of Wharf Street.

22 Dec **Jacob's Bazaar**: probably the Market Bazaar between Belgrave Gate and Mansfield Street.

29 Dec **Market Overton**: village near Oakham in Rutland.

Witham refers to the village of South Witham in Lincolnshire.

1 Jan 1884 **Osgodby**: village in Lincolnshire, near Market Rasen.

FURTHER READING

Elliott M., Victorian Leicester (1979)

Ellis C., History in Leicester (1948)

Read R., Modern Leicester (1881)

Simmons J., Life in Victorian Leicester (1971)

Leicester Past and Present, Vol. Two (1974)

"Mid-Victorian Leicester", *Transactions of the Leics. Archaeological & Historical Society, Vol. XLI* (1965-6)